THE

CASE

OF

GEORGE W. NIVEN, Esq.
Attorney and Counsellor at Law.

CHARGED WITH MAL-PRACTICES, AND SUSPENDED
BY ORDER OF THE

Court of Common Pleas,

OF THE

CITY OF NEW-YORK,

CONTAINING MUCH CURIOUS MATTER, INGENUOUS ARGU-
MENT, AND ELOQUENT DISCOURSE, EQUALLY IN-
TERESTING TO COUNSELLORS AND CLIENTS,
TO THE SAFETY OF THE PUBLIC, AND
THE HONOR AND DIGNITY OF
A LEARNED PROFESSION.

REPORTED BY
WILLIAM SAMPSON, Esq.
Counsellor at Law, &c.

New Introduction by Michael Hoeflich
*John H. & John M. Kane Professor of Law,
University of Kansas School of Law*

THE LAWBOOK EXCHANGE, LTD.
Clark, New Jersey

ISBN 9781616190255 (hardcover)
ISBN 9781616190262 (paperback)

Lawbook Exchange edition 2011

The quality of this reprint is equivalent to the quality of the original work.

THE LAWBOOK EXCHANGE, LTD.
33 Terminal Avenue
Clark, New Jersey 07066-1321

Please see our website for a selection of our other publications and fine facsimile reprints of classic works of legal history:
www.lawbookexchange.com

Library of Congress Cataloging-in-Publication Data

Sampson, William, 1764-1836.
  The case of George W. Niven, Esq. charged with mal-practices, and suspended by order of the Court of common pleas, of the city of New-York, containing much curious matter, ingenuous argument, and eloquent discourse, equally interesting to counsellors and clients, to the safety of the public, and the honor and dignity of a learned profession / reported by William Sampson, with a new introduction by Michael Hoeflich.
    p. cm.
  Previously published: New York : Van Pelt & Spears, 1829.
  Includes bibliographical references.
  ISBN-13: 978-1-61619-025-5 (hardcover : alk. paper)
  ISBN-10: 1-61619-025-6 (hardcover : alk. paper)
  ISBN-13: 978-1-61619-026-2 (pbk. : alk. paper)
  ISBN-10: 1-61619-026-4 (pbk. : alk. paper)
  1. Niven, George W. Trials, litigation, etc. 2. Trials (Malpractice)--New York (State)--New York. 3. New York (State). Court of Common Pleas (City and County of New York) I. Hoeflich, Michael H. II. Title.
  KF223.N58S36 2009
  347.747'05041--dc22
                                        2009045054

Printed in the United States of America on acid-free paper

INTRODUCTION

Michael Hoeflich*

George Niven was a scoundrel. He preyed upon some of society's most vulnerable people. His victims were petty criminals: prostitutes, pickpockets, and small time thieves incarcerated in one of the worst prisons of the era, New York City's aptly named "Tombs." He cheated his victims by promising them legal help and taking their meager property in exchange. He never provided the promised assistance but he certainly took their property. In many respects, Niven was a far worse criminal than his clients. He conspired with his victim's jailers to be introduced to them and he stole from them such small things as a prostitute's trunk of clothes or some poor furnishings from a pickpocket's room. He was nothing more than an amoral pettifogger whose actions contributed to the general popular dissatisfaction with lawyers and the law. Niven would have disappeared into the obscurity of insignificance and his name would not be known today but for the fact that William Sampson, Irish rebel, lawyer, and champion of codification, chose to publish a stenographic report of Niven's trial.

William Sampson was born in Londonderry in Ireland in 1764.[1] He qualified as a barrister, but his legal career in his home country took second place to his political activism

---

* John H. & John M. Kane Professor of Law, University of Kansas School of Law, 2009.
1. Biographical details about Sampson are drawn from *Memoirs of William Sampson including particulars of his adventures in*

THE CASE OF GEORGE W. NIVEN, ESQ.

in favor of Irish rights and defense of the Society of United Irishmen, a radical group. He took some part in the Uprising of 1798 and was apprehended by British forces as a result. During the next eight years he traveled to France and Portugal where he spent most of his time imprisoned. Finally, in 1806 he sailed for the United States and arrived there on the Fourth of July. Once established in New York City Sampson rapidly gained a forensic reputation and was active at the New York Bar. He also used his skills as a stenographer to prepare transcripts of a number of trials for publication. Often these trials featured Sampson himself as the successful lawyer. Sampson's most famous forensic effort was his representation in 1810 of the defendants in the *Trial of the Journeymen Cordwainers of New York City*,[2] one of the first American employee strike cases. His published version of the case undoubtedly contributed both to his fame and his fortune. His reputation as a radical jurist was confirmed by his publications and lectures

---

various parts of Europe, his confinement in the dungeons of theinquisition in Lisbon, &c., &c. : several original letters, being his correspondence with the ministers of state in Great-Britain and Portugal : a short sketch of the history of Ireland, particularly as it respects the spirit of British domination in that country : and a few observations on the state of manners, &c in America (N.Y.: Geo. Forman, 1807); Charles Currier Beale, *William Sampson. Lawyer and Stenographer* (Boston: N.Y.S. Stenographers Association, 1907); Irving Browne; "William Sampson," *The Green Bag* v. 8, pp. 313-325 (1896).

2. *Trial of the Journeymen Cordwainers of the City of New-York for a conspiracy to raise their wages: with the arguments of council ..., the verdict of the jury, and the sentence of the court* (N.Y.: Riley, 1807).

INTRODUCTION

advocating codification and Sampson was, in many ways, as important to the codification movement in the United States as was Bentham.[3]

In the same year as his defense in and publication of the Trial of the Journeymen Cordwainers Sampson undertook the defense of James Cheetham for an alleged libel he had published in his biography of Tom Paine.[4] Sampson published a stenographic transcript of this trial as well and featured his own oratory as the centerpiece of the work.[5] In 1818 Sampson was counsel in a somewhat bizarre case, the transcript of which he titled *Is a Whale a Fish?*[6] This was an early case which turned on scientific testimony and was probably partially responsible for bringing the theories of Carl Linnaeus to a broader readership.

The publication of George Niven's trial in 1822 seems to have been the last trial transcript reported by Sampson, a fact most likely attributable to his departure from New

---

3. See, M.W. Bloomfield, "William Sampson and the Codifiers: The Roots of American Legal Reform, 1820-1830," *American Jl. of Leg. Hist.* v.11, pp. (1967); W.J. Walsh, "Redefining Radicalism: A Historical Perspective," *Geo. Wash. L. Rev.* v.59, pp. 636-682 (1990-1991).
4. James Cheetham, *The Life of Thomas Paine* ( ).
5. *Speech of Counsellor Sampson, on the trial of James Cheetham, for libelling Madame Bonneville, in his Life of Thomas Paine with a short sketch of the trial* (N.Y.: Holt, 1810).
6. *Is a whale a fish? : an accurate report of the case of James Maurice against Samuel Judd, tried in the Mayor's Court of the city of New York, on the 30th and 31st of December 1818 : wherein the above problem is discussed theologically, scholastically, and historically* (N.Y.: C.S. van Winkle, 1819).

THE CASE OF GEORGE W. NIVEN, ESQ.

York to Washington soon after. Sampson did not appear as a lawyer in Niven's trial and we may suppose that he chose to report and publish the trial simply because it promised to be popular among the readers of such works. It had all the elements necessary to attract a wide audience: a corrupt lawyer, victims on the margins of society, and venal jail keepers. The trial, like most of those reported by Sampson, took place in the Mayor's Court in New York City and involved detailed testimonies by affidavit from several of Niven's victims. The trial resulted in a verdict of guilty against Niven. His punishment was to be struck off the list of attorneys in New York, an entirely appropriate, if not too mild, punishment for such a predatory lawyer.

The Trial of George W. Niven, Esq. is an important document in the legal, literary, and social history of the United States. As an example of popular literature it stands as representative of one of the most significant genres of antebellum literature. Beginning in the eighteenth century and continuing well into the nineteenth, reports of both real and fantasy trials were very popular among the growing number of literate Americans and Britons.[7] Pamphlets such as this were squarely in the tradition of popular criminal broadsides and narratives in periodicals and presaged the rise of detective stories first pioneered by E.A. Poe in the

---

7. Sampson himself contributed to this genre; see, *A faithful report of the trial of Hurdy Gurdy tried and convicted of a seditious libel in the Court of King's Bench, on the testimony of French Horn, the approver : with the arguments of counsel, and the charge of the learned chief justice to the jury* (N.Y.: B. Dornin, 1806).

INTRODUCTION

United States and Eugene Vidocq in France.[8] These early trial reports were inexpensive and, for the most part would have been seen as entertaining by potential readers.

As a source of legal history Sampson's report is triply significant. First it is an early source for the history of legal malpractice litigation in the U.S. Second, it provides a detailed description of the practice of a lawyer at the margins of the profession, one whose actions would have contributed to the generally low popular opinion of the legal profession at the time. The report also provides vital information about the daily lives of those who suffered imprisonment for crimes in the early Republic.

Although *The Trial of George Niven, Esq.* has been cited in the literature of antebellum law by a number of scholars it remains a relatively obscure work which few historians have actually read. This is most unfortunate and one may hope that its republication here will bring it to the greater prominence it deserves.

---

8. See, H. Worthington, *The Rise of the Detective in Early Nineteenth-Century Fiction* (N.Y. :Palgrave, 2005)

THE
CASE

OF

GEORGE W. NIVEN, Esq.
Attorney and Counsellor at Law.

CHARGED WITH MAL-PRACTICES, AND SUSPENDED
BY ORDER OF THE

Court of Common Pleas,

OF THE

CITY OF NEW-YORK,

CONTAINING MUCH CURIOUS MATTER, INGENUOUS ARGU-
MENT, AND ELOQUENT DISCOURSE, EQUALLY IN-
TERESTING TO COUNSELLORS AND CLIENTS,
TO THE SAFETY OF THE PUBLIC, AND
THE HONOR AND DIGNITY OF
A LEARNED PROFESSION.

REPORTED BY
WILLIAM SAMPSON, Esq.
Counsellor at Law, &c.

NEW YORK:
VAN PELT & SPEAR, PRINTERS, 95 PEARL-STREET.

1822.

Case, &c.

At the Court of General Sessions, held in January 1822, the Grand Jury made a presentment in writing to the Court, against George W. Niven, Esq. Counsellor at Law of the Supreme Court, as follows, to wit.

To the Honourable the Recorder and Aldermen, composing the Court of General Sessions, in and for the City and County of New-York.

The Grand Inquest, held in and for the Body of the City and County of New-York, on the 17th day of January 1822.

RESPECTFULLY PRESENT,

That complaints have been laid before them during their present Session, charging George W. Niven, Attorney and Counsellor at Law, with practices of a highly dishonourable nature, in visiting the Bridewell, and by falsehood and misrepresentation, inducing prisoners there confined, to employ him as counsel, in their defence, requiring of them money as fees for promised services, and when the persons were unable to advance it, prevailing on them to deposit in his custody, clothes and other property to a much larger amount, as security for the payment of such fees, which property he has subsequently refused to deliver to the individuals whom he has thus deluded.

The circumstances which have given rise to these charges are fully set forth in the annexed affidavits of Frederick Stivers, William Charley, and Alexander Kerland, and the Grand Jury are constrained to add, that information derived from authentic sources leaves no room to doubt, that this individual has been long habituated to similar misdemeanors.

It is a subject of great regret that while the nature of the testimony adduced in support of the accusations, has fully satisfied the Grand Jury of their truths, they do not come within the pale of an indictment for fraud, or obtaining money under false pretences.

They conceived themselves called upon however, in the discharge of their highly responsible duties to the great community, whose tranquility and honour, are for the time confided to their care, to solicit the immediate interference of your honors, in causing the name of the said George W. Niven to be stricken from the list of members of the New-York Bar, considering his longer continuance there, as a reproach upon the character of that learned and respectable body, and that measures may be taken to compel him to make ample restitution to the individuals who have been made the victims of his mal-practice.

Signed in behalf and at the unanimous request of the Grand Jury.

(Signed) JAS. B. MURRAY, *Secretary.*
(Signed) HERMAN THORN, *Foreman.*

The Grand Jury was composed of the following gentlemen.

GRAND JURY.

Thomas Thorn, *Foremen.*

Nicholas C. Everitt,	Kenlock Stewart,
Samuel Abrams,	John Johnson,
Stephen Gould,	George L. Ulshoeffer,
Thomas F. Livingston,	John M'Clure,
Francis Barett, jun.	James B. Murray,
Thomas M. Huntingdon,	Alexander Hossack,
Mathew Caroll,	James Palmer,
Samuel Norsworthy,	Henry Havens,
Samuel Packwood,	Benjamin Deforest,
Henry P. Beers,	John Perrot,
George Puffer,	Amos Butler.

This Presentment was filed the 17th January, and the following order was made by the Court of Sessions.

Ordered, by this Court, that the Clerk thereof, transmit the said Presentment and the affidavits accompanying the same to the Supreme Court.

In pursuance of the above order, they were delivered by Richard Hatfield, Esq. Clerk of the Court of Sessions, in person into the hands of the Chief Justice at Albany, after the January term. In May following, the Supreme Court, sitting in the city of New-York, made the following order, as appears by the endorsement of the Chief Justice, on the presentment.

The Supreme Court think it fit and most proper, under all the circumstances, that the matter of complaint against G. W. Niven, should be heard in the Mayor's Court, and they accordingly direct that these papers be handed to Judge Irving.

By the Court, A. SPENCER, *Chief Justice.*

May 6, 1822.

The three affidavits which accompanied the presentment were as follows :

CITY AND COUNTY OF NEW-YORK, SS.

Frederick Stivers, being duly sworn, does depose and say, that in the early part of this present month of December, he together with several other persons were taken up and committed to Bridewell on a charge of stealing and defrauding Messrs Colgates of Dutch-street, Tallow Chandlers, of tallow, soap fat, &c. &c. This deponent made a confession of all the circumstances to the police, and was told that he would be made a witness in the case. But while in Bridewell, in the upper hall, in a room with one Davis, he Davis, advised him the deponent to employ lawyer Niven, as he Niven was as good a lawyer as he could get, and done all the business for persons confined in Bridewell, also, telling deponent that he ought not to have told any thing about it, as Colgate and the police, would get out of him what they could, and then after all convict him. Niven used to call there to see Davis and enquire from him whether any new ones had come in, and if any strangers had been committed, they were recommended by Davis to Niven and deponent had a conversation with the said Niven, and told him that he did not want any counsel, to which, Niven replied, that if a prisoner's case was ever so bad, he wanted counsel; that Colgate and the police would make all the use of him they could, and convict him after all.

A few days after this, deponent was removed down in the lower hall, and was there told by Milligan, the bank robber, David Burger, and other prisoners, that he was a great fool for having confessed any thing; that Colgate and the police only wanted to get out of him what they could, and then convict him, as had been the case with others, and they advised deponent to employ Mr. Niven, and as he had no money, to give him an order for some of his furniture, as it would be as safe with Niven as to remain, as Colgate might get it all, after convicting him. Niven being in the habit of coming there two or three times a day after the prisoners, he had a conversation with the prisoners about his case. Burger again mentioned his business, and Niven then offered his services as counsel, saying, that it was necessary for every man to have counsel, let his case be ever so bad; that he had got several clear that were as guilty as the devil, and mentioned over several names. Deponent told Niven that he had no money, and he, Niven, then asked whether he, deponent, could not give him something as a fee of twenty-five dollars. Deponent then offered him a silver watch, which Niven said was too little ; after which an order was written by Milligan for a curled maple bedstead and a mahogany table, and a silver watch, which order was then handed to said Niven, who promised to keep the articles till he received his fee of twenty five dollars. The morning following, as Niven was talking to deponent, Mr. Sickles, the keeper, came by, and said that there was no use for him, Niven, to do any thing for deponent, as he was fully convicted already, or words to that import, whereupon Niven said, do you hear that: I told you, so now you see that you want a counsel, and I will try to get you clear. A few days after, Mr. Boorman, a friend of deponent, got him bail from prison, since which, deponent was advised to go to Mr Niven and ask for the articles received on the order, and offer him five dollars for his trouble, as he had not any trouble in particular as deponent knows of. Niven refused to take five dollars, and also refused to give up the watch and table, saying, that he, deponent, might have the bedstead, which was, accordingly, taken by deponent. This deponent further saith, that he would not have employed any counsel in consequence of the promise of Mr. Colgate and the police, had it not been for the repeated solicitations of Mr. Niven, that it was the intention of Mr. Colgate and the police to get out of him all they could, and then convict him after all.

his
Frederick × Stivers.
mark

Sworn the 28th of December, 1821. H. Abell.

CITY AND COUNTY OF NEW-YORK, SS.

Alexander Kerland of No. 50 Catharine Street, being duly sworn, doth depose and say, that about four months since this deponent was apprehended and taken to the police office, in consequence of counterfeit money being found in a house where this deponent accidently was, at the time the marshalls entered the said house, and this deponent further saith, that he was searched in the police office, and from thence was committed to Bridewell for examination. That on the next day, or the day after, George W. Niven, attorney at law, introduced himself to this deponent, who told this deponent, that he, the said Niven, could get him out that day, as he, Niven, had great interest with the police. That if deponent remained there, he would go to the state prison, all of which had a tendency to alarm this deponent, not then knowing that it was intended to extort money from this deponent, and this deponent further saith, that the said Niven asked this deponent five dollars in cash to get him out of prison, but as this deponent had not the money; the said Niven asked ten dollars, to be paid at some future day, and security being put in the hands of the said Niven accordingly, this deponent gave the said Niven an order upon Peter M'Arden for his trunk and contents, which was a variety of clothing, in value about thirty dollars, which the said Niven received; and this deponent further saith, that last night he called on the said Niven, and tendered or offered the ten dollars, and at the same time demanded the trunk and clothes, which the said Niven refused to deliver, alleging, that he received the trunk and clothes as a fee, and not as security for the payment of the ten dollars, by which means this deponent has been defrauded of his property, who is a poor man, who works hard as a brewer for five dollars and an half a week. And this deponent further saith, that when he was examined in the police office, and they made acquainted with the fact, that this deponent's being in the house before alluded to was altogether accidental, he was discharged, the said Niven was not present, nor does this deponent believe that the said Niven had any agency to effect the said discharge. Alexander Kerland.

Sworn before me this 16th day of January, 1822. H. Abell.

CITY AND COUNTY OF NEW-YORK, SS.

William Charley, No. 50 Catharine Street, being duly sworn, doth depose and say, that about four months since, he purchased of a negro man named Church, three razors, and paid him three shillings for the same. About two days after this, deponent was charged with purchasing the said razors, knowing them to be stolen, and was committed to bridewell. That while in bridewell, George W. Niven, attorney at law, introduced himself to this deponent, and told this deponent, that he, Niven, would clear this deponent for five dollars, when this deponent informed him he had not the money, the said Niven wished to know whether this deponent had any thing he could give as a pledge for the payment of the five dollars, and this deponent further saith, that he left a silver watch in the police office which cost this deponent four pounds 10 shillings, in Bristol, in England, about four years ago, when, at the instance of the said Niven, this deponent gave an order on the police office to deliver the said watch to the said Niven, which he, Niven, was to hold as security until this deponent paid him the five dollars, as aforesaid. And this deponent further saith, that a day or two after he had given the order as aforesaid, the said Niven came to this deponent in person, and told him that the police office would not deliver the watch; that this deponent was as guilty as all hell, and that all hell would not clear this deponent, or words to that effect, which induced this deponent to dispose of a fowling piece for six dollars, in order to pay the said Niven the five dollars, as aforesaid, lest this deponent should be convicted for the want of five dollars, and this deponent further saith, that he paid the said Niven the five dollars as aforesaid. In a day or two afterwards, the said Niven informed this deponent, that he had received the watch from the police office, since which, he has demanded the watch from the said Niven, who refuses to deliver it, and who uses violent and abusive language towards this deponent, calling him a drunken foreign villain, and threatened to   this deponent out of his house; at one time demanding from this deponent twenty-five dollars for the watch, and at another time refusing to let this deponent have the watch at all. By the means resorted to as aforesaid, this deponent, who is a poor man, has been defrauded of his watch.

William Charley.

Sworn before me this 16th day of January, 1822. H. *Abell.*

The Court of Common Pleas in compliance with the direction of the Supreme Court, accordingly proceeded to the investigation, and made the following order:

NEW-YORK, COMMON PLEAS, Monday, May 20, 1822.

In the matter of the presentment of the Grand Jury, against G. W. Niven, Esqr.

Ordered, that a copy of the presentment made by the Grand Inquest, held in and for the city and county of New-York, on the 17th of January, 1822, to the Court of General Sessions of the peace of the said city and county, held at the day and year aforesaid, against George W. Niven, Esq. and also a copy of the proceedings of said Court of Sessions, and also, of the Supreme Court upon the same presentment, be served upon the said George W. Niven: and let the said George W. Niven, show cause before this Court on the first day of June next, at the opening of the Court on that day, why he, should not be suspended from practicing as an attorney and counsellor of this court.

Court of Common Pleas, Saturday, June 1, 1822.

On this day Mr. Niven appeared with Messrs. Bogardus and Anthon, as his counsel, to show cause pursuant to the rule, and the court assigned Hugh Maxwell, Esq., District Attorney, and Martin S. Wilkins, Esq. to read the presentment, and conduct the proceedings against Mr. Niven, Mr. Maxwell, then read the presentment, and the three above affidavits accompanying it. Also the order of Stivers to his wife, and that of Kerland to Peter M'Ardle; and that given by Charley for his watch.

On behalf of Mr. Niven, Mr. Anthon read several affidavits to contradict or explain those of which the copies had been served. Mr. Maxwell then moved the court, that additional affidavits might be read against Mr. Niven, which was strongly opposed, whereupon it was ordered, that they should be first submitted to the court, and that copies of such as were deemed relevant, should be served on Mr. Niven or his counsel.

The affidavits read this day by Mr. Anthon on behalf of Mr. Niven, were the following, viz. Mr. George W. Niven's affidavit in answer to Stivers. Stivers's second affidavit. Mr. Nivens answer to Charley, the same as to Kerland, and the affidavit of H. K. Niven, as to Stiver's second affidavit, all of which will be found in the following pages. And Mr. Maxwell read a third affidavit of Stivers, which will be found in its proper place.

Saturday 12 o'clock, June 22, 1822.

The court now resumed the inquiry, and the order of proceeding established, was, that the assigned counsel should read the presentment and their affidavits without comment. The affidavits in answer to be then read in the same way. Then counsel should be heard, and that then Mr. Niven or his counsel should have the reply. And that if further time should be required after the court was possessed of all the facts, it should be allowed according to the circumstances and reason of the case. Mr. Maxwell, was accordingly proceeding to read the presentment, but was interrupted by the defendants counsel, who objected to its being read. They said the presentment had already been considered by the court as a nullity, and that the case was to be taken up as an original inquiry before an independent court. That it was a hardship upon Mr. Niven to be tried not by peers, but by affidavits of persons not subjected to the test of cross-examination, nor to responsibility in case of falsehood or perjury; to be put in jeopardy by the mere finding of a grand jury upon ex party testimony, which was itself but hearsay, and no evidence of any thing. When a man is tried upon an indictment, it is read as containing the charge, but never used as evidence. It is a thing to be proved by evidence, but is not evidence.

This they said was the first time that any individual had been presented as a nuisance. If this be established in the case of a counsellor, it will follow of course, that judges, justices, and magistrates of every kind will be subject to the same regimen, Things that are noxious to public health, morals, or convenience, may be presented as nuisances, but not persons. This had never before been attempted but in one case, that of William Smith, and then it was disregarded and fell to the ground. It would be hard to foresee, and impossible to foretell the mischiefs that might follow from countenancing such scandalous presentments.

The court ruled that the presentment should be read, but that they would found their decisions entirely upon the evidence independantly of it.

The counsel then asked if they were held to answer the presentment, or the affidavits accompanying it only, and were told by the court, that they were to answer all of which they had copies served, according to the rule. The presentment was then read by Mr. Maxwell, and the three foregoing affidavits which accompanied it. Mr. Maxwell, also, read the following affidavits.

CITY OF NEW-YORK, ss.

Edward Couhenhoven, at present living in the town of Greenburgh, county of West-Chester, being duly sworn, says, that about five years ago, as near as he can recollect, he purchased rising of one hundred cords of wood from Abraham Barker, then living in the county of Rockland, the wood to be delivered in the highlands. That deponent afterwards sent up two sloops, and had all but about six cords taken away. The six cords remained there till the following spring. In the fall previous to taking away the wood, deponent was on his passage up to Albany, and stopped in the Highlands, nearly opposite to where the remaining part of the wood lay. And there, *Baker*, together with a Mr. Chatterton and others, eat dinner with deponent, on board of the vessel. While so on board, Baker asked why the wood was not taken away, viz. the said six cords which they saw laying through the cabin windows. Deponent said he intended to take it on his return, but did not, and left it to the following spring, as aforesaid. After taking the wood, he received a letter from one Stevens, demanding payment for the said wood, for which deponent was shortly afterwards prosecuted in the Marine Court in this city. On going to the court to defend the case, he fell in with George W. Niven, Esq. and stated to him the case, and paid him a fee for going up and attending to the case. After the case was tried, the Justice said he would take time to give his judgment, and deponent was not permitted to depart the court without giving security to abide the judgment, and he was about to leave the sum of money claimed from him, which was about thirty-seven dollars and some cents, as surety, when said Niven told him not to leave the money, but to hand it to him, the said Niven, and keep them out of it as long as he could, and that he would attend to it, and pay it in case judgment should be given against him; at the same time saying, "don't humour the damned rascals so much." Deponent, thinking the said Niven would attend to it, and pay it in case the said judgment should be against him, handed said Niven forty dollars, as near as he can recollect, and then came away, leaving Niven to manage it. He, the winter following, viz. about three years since, as near as he now recollects, he received a letter requesting him to come and pay the judgment and costs or he would be prosecuted. He came down, and went and saw Niven, and he, Niven, abused deponent, and pretended to make out an account against him which would set off, or meet the said forty dollars, and refused to refund or pay any part of the said forty dollars. Deponent further says, that he then went and paid the judgment and costs, which, in effect, was paying for the wood three times. Deponent further says, that the said Niven yet retains, and unjustly holds, the money from him, and has no claim or demand whatever, to the knowledge of this deponent, on said money, or any part thereof: and further says not.

Edward Couhenhoven.

Sworn the 24th of May, 1822. *James Hopson, Justice.*

CITY OF NEW-YORK, SS.

John I. Shoemaker, of No. 19 Murray Street, merchant, being duly sworn, says, that in the month of November last, a man by the name of George Peers, was committed to Bridewell on a charge of stealing a coat. In December following, at the request of the brother of said Peers, deponent spoke to George W. Niven, Esq. counsel for the said Peers, requesting him to have the trial put off till the next term, and, at the same time, deponent was asked by the said Niven to become bail for the said Peers, and would see deponent again on the subject. A few days after deponent met with said Niven, and they had a conversation about it, in which Niven said, that he could have the bail reduced to one hundred and fifty, or two hundred dollars, and after said Peers should be out on bail, deponent had better advise him to runaway, and in case the bail should be called on, that he (Niven) would petition the Court of Exchequer and have the same discharged, or words to that import. Deponent said he would consider of it, but nothing further was done till the following term, when the said Peers was called out for trial, at which time said Niven went up to Peers and spoke to him, and presently said Peers plead guilty to the charge, and was afterwards sent to the penitentiary. Niven after the conversation had with him, told deponent, that he did not want any thing said about it.

John I. Shoemaker.

Sworn 4th of April, 1822. *H. Abell, Special Justice.*

CITY OF NEW-YORK, SS.

Ellen Griffin of No. 244, Cherry-Street, at Mrs. Adam's being duly sworn, says, that on or about the first of October last, she was taken up in Walnut-Street, and committed to bridewell, and from there went to the penitentiary for six months. While in bridewell and previous to her being sent to the penitentiary, she saw, and spoke to a lawyer by the name of George W. Niven, who wears spectacles, for him to try to get her out, or get her term shortened, and she would give him ten dollars, and give him security for the money as she had not the cash. He (Niven,) said that he would do the best he could, and she accordingly gave him an order or power to get her trunk of clothes, and a leghorn hat and keep the same as security for the money. She went to the penitentiary, and served six months out, as Niven did not get her out. And after her term had expired she went to get her clothes, and found that her lawyer Niven had got the trunk containing clothes of the value of about fifteen dollars, and her hat of the value of about fifteen dollars. She then went to Niven, and saw him about it, and he said that he had got the trunk and clothes and hat. The hat he said he had given away to a poor girl, and as to the other articles she must call again, and he would let her know about it. That she has seen him once since and he said he was engaged and that she must call again, and she has called once since but did not see him.

her
Ellen × Griffin.
mark

Sworn the 27th of May, 1822.   R. Ricker.

CITY OF NEW-YORK, SS.

Thomas M. Collins, a marshall, being duly sworn, says, that about the first of October last, as near as he can recollect, he arrested Ellen Griffin, the person above-named, and brought her to the police office, and she was sent to the penitentiary for six months. Shortly after, George W. Niven, Esq. called on him with a power of attorney from Ellen, to get her trunk and clothing, and hat, &c. A suit was commenced for the articles, but before the trial the articles were given up, and the property taken to the house of said Niven, by deponent, at his (Niven's) request, and for which deponent received from a dollar, to one dollar and fifty cents, for his trouble. An inventory of the articles was made out, and put into the trunk by this deponent, and he really thinks, that the whole of the property was worth from twenty-five to thirty dollars, and further deponent says not.

Thomas M. Collins.

Sworn the 27th of May, 1822, before me.   R. Riker.

CITY OF NEW-YORK, SS.

Thomas M. Collins above named, being duly sworn, says, that the inventory hereto annexed is the one above spoken of, and he this morning obtained the same from George W. Niven, Esq., on

whom he called by the directions of Ellen Griffin, to obtain the property and pay him five dollars for any trouble he might have had; Niven stated that the articles were his, and that she (Ellen) might do as she pleased, and go to h—l or words to that effect, but he finally said, that as the five dollars was something, although nothing in comparison for the trouble he had had, she might have them, if she would take them as they were, and he took deponent up stairs and there showed him several articles, among which was the hat which had been dyed and cut up, which articles deponent then refused to take, in the condition in which they were, and further says not. Thomas M. Collins.
Sworn the 28th of May, 1822. J. Hedden.

Inventory.—One black veil, two open gowns white, one muslin frock, one black silk ditto, one flannel petticoat, two diaper towels, one morning gown, one night cap, one black feather, three ruffles and vandike, three peices of curtain, one work bag contents of trimming, one bonnet and trimmed with plaid ribbon, and one handkerchief.

CITY OF NEW-YORK, SS.

Robert Latimer of No. 145, Hudson-Street, being duly sworn, says, that in the year 1818, as near as he can judge, and previous to the marriage of Mary Sarah Holman the daughter of deponent with Isaac Clason, she (Mary,) gave deponent a writing, whereby it was understood that deponent should keep and protect her furniture and property, consisting of bedding, sideboard, tables, looking glasses, carpeting, chairs, piano forte, gold watch, &c. for the benefit of her child Josephine Holman. (she and her child living with deponent at the time) in case, she (Mary) should die or get married. After her marriage with Clason, he demanded the before mentioned property from deponent as his right by marriage, which deponent refused to give up, and was prosecuted for ten thousand dollars damages. Deponent called on Jeremiah J. Drake, Esq to defend the suit &c., but Drake declined it saying, that he did not wish to, in consequence of some family business, and said that he would recommend a person, and accordingly a few days afterwards called on deponent in company with Doctor Ben. Kissam, now or late of the navy, and George W. Niven, Esq., and introduced deponent to Niven as the lawyer who would attend to the business. Niven accordingly undertook the same and advised deponent to give a bond and judgment, in order to save the property from Clason, which judgment was to be void on the payment of two hundred dollars to Messrs. Whitson and Place, two hundred dollars to said Doctor Kissam, and two hundred and fifty dollars to said Niven or thereabouts, although deponent was not as he verily believes indebted to Kissam little or nothing, and to Niven not a single cent, and not over one hundred and fifty dollars as he thinks to Whitson and Place, and upon the sale of the property he (Niven,) was to have some person or persons to bid the same in for the benefit of the child Josephine Holman. Niven also, advised deponent to go to the surrogate, and there in company with Doctor Kissam, offered to become the guardian, so as more effectually to protect the property for the child. Deponent however offered himself to become the guardian, but did not, and during this business Niven called on deponent for fifty dollars, which he said he must have for court fees &c., and deponent not having the money, gave him a gold watch which cost upwards of one hundred dollars, as security for the money, saying, that that was the watch of the child. Deponent at the same time made Niven a present of a gold watch seal for his politeness, which cost three guineas. Niven at the same time said that he would return the watch on the payment of the fifty dollars, and wrote a paper to that effect as deponent supposed, which he deponent signed, which fifty dollars was afterwards paid to Niven by Mr. Bartlett, then justice of the 6th ward court, but the watch has not to this day been returned, neither the money, but it is now worn by said Niven as deponent believes.

The household furniture, such as before mentioned, which was in the house, and the whole of which was the property left as aforesaid for the child, were sold under the execution issued on the judgment as aforesaid for a mere trifle, as Niven mentioned at the time, that the sale was only intended for the benefit of the child, by which many persons declined bidding on them. After the sale, Niven stated, that the property was his as he had had it all bid in, and he took away a piano forte, a set of cut-glass, decanters, tumblers, and wines, two large china water-jugs, a pair of andirons, a large mahogany dining table, and hall lamp, with its appendages, &c. in all, as deponent supposes, worth about four hundred dollars. Deponent still believing, that it was all done for the benefit of the child, all of which property and money is yet unaccounted for and unsettled, but detained, part in the possession of Niven, and part with Doctor Kissam, by which, deponent, and the child, as aforesaid, have been defrauded thereof as aforesaid, and that Whitson and Place become paid by the purchase of the property in deponent's ... . And, afterwards, when said Niven was spoken to, to settle the same, he refused, as deponent understood, and not being satisfied with getting the property in the manner aforesaid, prevailed on the security of deponent (as he, deponent, has been informed) to surrender him, which was done, and he had to procure other bail at the suit of said Clason.

Robert Latimer.

Sworn before me, the 31st of May, 1822. J. Hedden, Special Justice.

City of New-York, ss.

John Davenport, of Washington Market, butcher, being duly sworn, says, that last spring two years ago, as near as he recollects, George W. Niven, Esq. then living in what is now called Fulton-Street, was in the practice of dealing with deponent, and being indebted to deponent in a small sum, he employed him (Niven) to prosecute a man by the name of Bronson, of Orange County, for damages about a pair of cattle purchased from him by deponent. The suit was finally tried by the sheriff's jury, and deponent recovered about sixty dollars, as near as he recollects. Deponent not wishing to injure Bronson's security, undertook to collect the money himself from Bronson, in Orange County, and got the judgment, or necessary documents from Niven, for that purpose, and sent a man up. viz. a Mr. Fountain, to collect it. About this time, or not long after, George W. Niven received an account against deponent to collect, amounting to about thirty dollars, as he thinks, which he wanted deponent to pay, but which he (deponent) said he could not then pay, but that if he (Niven) would settle with him, (having, during the time, at different times, got beef from deponent) he would try and pay the account, as there could not be much wanting from deponent ; Niven replied, that he did not think that he owed deponent any thing, and requested deponent to make out his bill, and that he (Niven) would pay if there was any thing due from him, but before deponent made out the account, he was prosecuted on the account of D. Bedell, for which judgment was given against deponent, and for which he went on the limits, and while so on the limits, he called on Niven, with the account made out, amounting to fifty-six dollars, as he thinks, and Niven produced his account against it, amounting to about sixty-two dollars and some cents, which deponent could not dispute, as he knew nothing about it, telling Niven, however, that a man had better not sue if the costs came to more than the debt, or words to that import. They then walked down to the market, and there deponent mentioned it to a butcher, saying, that the costs had come to more than the debt. Niven hearing it, called deponent a damned liar, saying that it was not so ; but that it was for counsel fees, as well as the costs, having given him counsel about lands in Cincinnati, which deponent told him was not true, as he never had any lands in Cincinnati, and, therefore, could not want counsel, and that he had not done any other business other than that before mentioned, and so they then parted. Deponent, afterwards, thinking that he, Niven, was not entitled to so much as he had charged, sued him in the Marine Court, and there Niven set off his costs, and the demand that he made against deponent, but judgment was given against Niven for upwards of twenty-six dollars, as near as he recollects. After the commencement of this suit, and previous to the trial, Niven told deponent that he did not want to spend money in costs, and that he would leave it to a Mr. M'Donald, the attorney of deponent, and, accordingly, the time was appointed to see M'Donald. The morning following this conversation, Niven, and his brother, came to the market, and Niven asked deponent if he was ready to go, to which he replied, " directly." Niven then said that he would step down in the country market, and on his return they would go, and then he, Niven, and his brother, left deponent, and in a few minutes G. W. Niven returned, and took hold of deponent by the arm, and said " now let us go," and they started to go, and as they were passing Fulton-Street, deponent stopped short, saying, that he could not go, as it was off the limits; Niven answered him, saying, there is no danger " as long as you are with me," and deponent was finally persuaded to go; they remained in M'Donald's office sometime, talking over the business, but M'Donald said that he could not then attend to it, but that they could go up to the court and have the suit adjourned. They then came out, and on coming up to Greenwich-Street deponent wanted to go to Fulton Street, but Niven held on to him, saying he wanted to stop at the livery stable of Dawson, at the head of the street. Deponent replied, that Dawson had moved, and Niven replied, "never mind," there is some body there, or words to that effect, as he wanted to get a horse to ride out; they, accordingly, came up, and Niven made some stay at the stable, when they came out, and came up to Broadway, and so up to the hall. Between Dey and Fulton Street they were met by the brother of Niven, who had left the market as aforesaid, who was in company with an officer, with whom George W. Niven stopped, and had some conversation while deponent passed on. In the park George W. Niven overtook deponent, and they went and had the suit adjourned. This was the day that the lawyers were summing up Goodwin's case. When deponent returned to the market, he was told that his surety had been sued for his being off the limits, and the day following, deponent was informed that said George W Niven had made his boast, that he had fixed a plan to get or catch deponent off of the limits, had succeeded, and he gloried in it. After which deponent refused to settle with him, and got judgment as aforesaid. On the trial for the escape of deponent from the limits, he (deponent) stated the whole of the circumstances, and Niven, under oath, denied ever having told him that he could or would not be hurt, but to the contrary, had said, " that that was his business." The Court, after hearing the whole of the case, gave judgment in favour of deponent's security. And further says not. John Davenport.

Sworn the 29th of May, 1822. *H. Abell.*

CITY OF NEW-YORK, SS.

Samuel W. Jennings, of 288 Greenwich-Street, hatter, being duly sworn, says, that last fall a year ago, and during the trial of Mr. Goodwin, deponent was present in the store of George Hodgson, in Washington-Street, when George W. Niven, Esq., stated that he had laid a plan to get or catch a person off the limits, and that he had succeeded and gloried in so doing, and on his being asked who it was that he had so caught, answered *that it was John Davenport.*

Samuel W. Jennings.

Sworn the 30th of May, 1822. *J. Hedden.*

Stiver's 2d affidavit formerly read by Mr. Anthon.

The second affidavit of Stivers, read on the 1st of June, in behalf of Mr. Niven, in answer to his first, which accompanied the presentment, is here inserted for the better understanding of the third, which was this day read by Mr. Maxwell.

CITY OF NEW-YORK, SS.

Frederick Stivers, of the City of New-York, being duly sworn, saith, that he was arrested and put in the bridewell of this city, charged with stealing, that on being committed he was advised by some of his fellow prisoners to employ counsel, and was recommended to employ George W. Niven, Esq. as his counsel. That he this deponent did employ Mr. Niven as his counsel, and did agree to pay him a fee of twenty-five dollars. That deponent gave Mr. Niven an order on his nephew, in Pearl Street, for the money, that shortly after Mr. Niven and deponents nephew came to the prison, and deponents nephew told deponent. that the property and money which he should have of deponent was covered, and was to be handed over by an order from deponent to Mr. Colgate, which he had accepted. Deponent proposed to Mr. Niven, to secure him his fee of twenty five dollars, in property he did not want, and that if he should get clear, he would redeem the same; Mr. Niven at first objected, and said he did not like to take property in that way, to secure fees: upon which deponent who was then fully committed, charged with grand larceny, urged Mr. Niven until he consented, and then deponent had an order drawn which deponent signed for Mr. Niven to receive of deponents wife as security. for his said fee of twenty-five dollars, which deponent had agreed to pay him, to wit; one tea table which was not in use, and which deponent had taken for rent, one single bedstead not in use, and one silver watch, chain and key. That deponent has since called on Mr. Niven for the bedstead as he wanted to use it, Mr. Niven though not under any obligation to do so, readily gave the bedstead and kept the rest as his security, and this deponent further saith, that the whole conduct of Mr. Niven was correct and satisfactory to him deponent, and deponent further saith, that he was sent for by Mr. Colgate to come to his house, when in a conversation Mr. Colgate told deponent to go to Mr. Hedden the next morning and see him. That deponent did accordingly go, and in the office under the direction of *this deponent*,* his deposition was taken, which he deponent does not know or recollect what it contained, but if there are any charges or allegations, against Mr. Niven, deponent did not mean that there should be, as there was no ground for the same, and further deponent saith not.

his
Frederick ⨯ Stivers.
mark

Sworn before me this 17th day of January, 1821. *John T. Irving.*

*Above the word " this deponent" was penciled above, " *Mr. Hedden,*" which was alledged to be the correction of a mistake.

Stivers's third affidavit, read by Mr. Maxwell in answer to the foregoing.

CITY OF NEW-YORK, ss.

Frederick Stivers of the city of New-York, being duly sworn, saith, that on the twenty-eighth day of December last past, this deponent made oath to an affidavit before Henry Abell Esq. Special Justice in the police Office of the said city, in relation to the conduct and behaviour of George W. Niven, Esq. towards this deponent, whilst he was confined in the city prison of the said city; which said affidavit, and the circumstances therein stated, are just and true. And this deponent further saith, that sometime in the month of January last, to the best of this deponent's recollection, and after he was discharged from confinement in the said city prison, he, this deponent was called upon by the said George W. Niven, in relation to the above mentioned affidavit, who was very anxious to have this deponent make another deposition concerning the circumstances in part therein set forth, which he the said Niven, said to deponent was necessary for him to do, and which would relieve him, the said Niven, from difficulty, and at the same time no injury would or could be done to this deponent, should he make another affidavit as aforesaid. And this deponent saith, that shortly thereafter the said Niven called upon deponent, with an affidavit as he said, and which he, the said Niven, read to deponent, (as he, this deponent, can neither read writing, nor write) and the said last mentioned affidavit, so read to him as aforesaid by the said Niven, not seeming to contradict the circumstances in the said affidavit by this deponent sworn to before Henry Abell, first above mentioned, this deponent was taken by the said Niven, before the honorable John T. Irving, Esq. at his office, in the City-Hall of the said city; before whom this deponent made oath to the said affidavit, drawn by the said Niven; and deponent further saith, that if the said affidavit last mentioned, contains any matter or thing whatever, by way of refuting or denying any matter or thing set forth or contained in the first deposition, made before the said Henry Abell, Esq. as aforesaid, then the said George W. Niven, Esq. did not read the same to him in truth and in good faith, as he, the said Niven, pretended to do. But in that case, the same is false, unjust, and untrue, and this deponent has there made oath to circumstances related in said affidavit, which were never at any time or place read to deponent by said Niven or any other person whatever.

his
Frederick ✕ Stivers.
mark

Sworn before me, this 1st April 1822. R. Riker.

Mr. Price wished the Court to pursue a different course, and rather to consider this as an application on behalf of Mr. Niven to quash the presentment. He admitted that it was difficult to find a precise rule of proceeding, as the case was without precedent. It was not like an indictment in which a definite charge is made of a specific cause, and the matter so set forth as that an issue can be taken upon it ; and the proof of that issue to be upon the accusing party. Here is a charge against George W. Niven, not as a citizen called upon to answer for any offence against the law, but as G. W. Niven, a counsellor of this Court, to answer for acts not relating to this court, nor for any crimes defined or known in our criminal jurisprudence. The judgment which is to deprive him of his livelihood, and his children of bread, to blacken his reputation, and utterly destroy him, is not to be the judgment of his peers, nor the law of the land, but a trial by affidavits, on charges which no other of our citizens could be put to answer. The magistrates who sit on this bench, are not the judges who usually sit here, though they may be entitled so to do. Their custom is to sit as associates with the judges of the criminal courts and not in this court to decide upon questions touching its dignity and discipline. And, again, the question is, whether Mr. Niven shall be struck off the rolls of this court, whilst, in all the affidavits, there is no one act of misfeasance, or malfeasance, which took place in this Court.

But, supposing the matter properly before this court, and the magistrates who now compose it, what should be the course of proceeding in the ordinary cases of an attorney detaining his clients money ? The rule is, that he pay over the money. He then knows what is required of him. But here he cannot be certain to what particular charge a particular answer may be required. It is not a single affidavit, or a single charge, but a complaint made out of eight or nine unconnected affidavits. Is it upon the general effect that may possibly be produced by the reading of all these affidavits, that he is to be struck off the roll, or is it from some one in particular ? Is it for going into the bridewell ? Is it for receiving from a prostitute a fee beyond what his standing authorized ? Is it because he charged a client twenty-five dollars ? If so, and persons not acquainted with his abilities may think he charged too much, I have only to say, that there are men of longer and higher standing, that would make out a bill of twice as much. Is it that he took the wearing apparel of the female ? He did not take money, for she had none to give him ; he had no choice but that or to give his time for nothing. If he took clothes, or beds, or bedsteads, he did what many of the profession would not do, but his poverty, and not his will might consent ; but what is there criminal in this, that should deprive him of his bread ? Misery makes us acquainted with strange bed fellows ; and it might be the case with others to stoop as low, had they not been more blessed by fortune. This prostitute fed him with her goods and chattels, to get her, if he could, a remission of her six month sentence. This fee he accepted ; and that is the crime imputed.

With respect to the services and charges in the Marine Court, that court has a roll of attorneys, and they practice there by licence of that court. It was there that mistakes or overcharges should have been examined, and errors rectified.

Mr. Maxwell observed here, that if this discourse was intended as going to the merits, it was premature, as he had something more to offer in the way of evidence.

Mr. Price. In this new case, a new order of proceeding has been struck out, but we are not to be deprived of the common right to be heard, and if I can satisfy the court that they cannot strike Mr Niven off the roll, it would amount to the same as an application to quash the proceedings, and the party will not be put to answer, by which means much time and pains will be saved. He then proceeded to examine the affidavits.

Couheuhoven was bail for a thief, and applied to Mr. Niven to be concerned for that thief, Mr Niven told him, that thief had better not stand trial. I have heard of such advice given by counsel, whom some would rank higher than Mr. Niven, though I should not have given this advice, yet it was not criminal upon the representations of the bail to say, that his principal ought not to risk a trial, but rather suffer the penalty of the law, for not doing so. Youth often moves such sympathy, and justice itself connives at it, and good men often wish, that even the guilty should not suffer for a first offence, and rather that the party should be bailed, and leave the country, than be put to shame and lasting degradation.

Mr. Davenport, was a butcher on the limits, Mr. Niven was concerned for a creditor, and if he did form the project of getting him off the limits, the whole amounted to this, that he wanted to make him pay a just debt. It was as one might say, "to do a great right, do a little wrong:" and besides there was another court competent to punish Mr. Niven, to whom it properly belonged, and it ought not to be drawn in question here. As to Mr. Latimer's affidavit, it charges an offence for which we show by a record, that Mr. Niven was already put upon his trial and acquitted. If this were an indictment he could plead *autrefois acquit*, for no man is to answer twice for any crime. He was tried before a judge of the Supreme Court. That judge might have struck him off the roll or represented him to the court of which he was a member. If this was not made a subject of inquiry in that court, why should it in this ? There is a portion of this community prejudiced beyond reason against lawyers ; and unfortunately there are members of the profession who have given some cause for that prejudice. This circumstance may have induced this court to establish this inquiry, but, however good the motive, the party should be fairly dealt with. Here is a presentment by a grand jury for a matter which they must have known from the public prosecutor was not an indictable offence, for which he could be put on his trial by the laws of this community. Yet it is put upon record with the names of twenty-four respectable individuals upon their oaths, and there it may remain forever, without any possibility on his part of bringing it to trial by a jury. Two thieves and a receiver, whom he meets with in the course of his practice in the criminal court, and who have malice against him, are the only witnesses : and they are not produced, nor cross-examined, nor confronted. Their hearsay testimony is made evidence against him by this novel proceeding, whereas, if he was on a legal trial the court would not so much as suffer them to open their lips in their presence, or if they did, they would be bound publicly to declare their own infamy upon their cross-examination.

Lawyers are not more than any other class of the community, to be put out of the pale of the law. Like other men, they have their failings, their vices, and their crimes; but they are not upon a footing of equality if the precedent be once established, that they can be presented by grand juries, and without a trial by their peers, stripped of their character and livelihood. I therefore submit it to the wisdom of this court, whether it will require any answer to this charge, or feel itself called upon or disposed to travel into other courts to hunt for grounds of special interference in matters which no way affect its own authority or dignity.

The first judge. This gentleman has been called upon to answer as a member of the profession, and an officer of this court, for his professional conduct, and all the judges of this court have been convened. They are also judges of the Court of Sessions, and this gentleman, in consequence of being licenced in this court, was admissible to practice there, there being no roll there, nor special admission of attorneys or counsel. We are all therefore interested in the conduct of this member of the bar, as well in the sessions, as in this court; we shall therefore proceed in the investigation, giving to the party a fair opportunity of being fully heard. We consider it salutary, and absolutely necessary for the pure and administration of justice, and we consider that there is enough presented to us to call upon him for an answer.

Mr. Anthon, wished to ascertain, whether the whole accusation was now before the court. At the last day of the examination, new charges were adduced. If the party is again put to answer new affidavits, he can never expect to come to an end.

Mr. Maxwell, said this could not now be positively answered. It must depend upon the facts disclosed by the other side, and the affidavits to be produced by them. We have affidavits disclosing other facts, similar to what the court have heard. If no new matters are stated by Mr. Niven in his defence, we ask no more time, nor to introduce any new charges, we have however others touching the facts already before the court.

Mr. Anthon. In the Supreme Court, when an attorney is called upon to answer charges upon affidavits, he brings in his affidavits, and then the matter rests. Why not so here?

Mr. Maxwell. Justice would not be done if the mere oath of the party charged with the transgression, was to stop all inquiry into the truth and merits of the case. And now for instance, if the evidence of Doctor Kissam be denied, we have his affidavit.

Mr. Bogardus. He was however as much implicated as Mr. Niven in that very matter.

The first judge. We cannot anticipate what may or may not, be necessary for our information, nor make any positive order at this moment.

Mr. Anthon. If it is understood that no new affidavit is to be produced, charging any new matter, we go on. He then read the following affidavits and documents.

CITY AND COUNTY OF NEW-YORK, SS.

George W. Niven, of the said city, being duly sworn, saith, that in the course of his professional duties, he visited the bridewell of this city to consult with his clients, who were there confined, when Frederick Stivers, in the annexed deposition* named, and who was then a prisoner in the upper hall of the said prison, applied to this deponent to become his counsel. On inquiry, this deponent ascertained, that said Stivers was not fully committed; in consequence of which, this deponent refused to consult with him until he was fully committed, which refusal originated from a rule adopted by the keeper of said prison, that counsel should not consult with their clients until they were fully committed. That, afterwards, this deponent had occasion to visit some clients of his in the lower hall of said prison, where the said Stivers had been transferred. That while this deponent was at the gates of the said prison, consulting with clients, who had previously retained this deponent, the said Stivers again applied to this deponent to employ him as his counsel, upon which, the keeper, Mr. Sickles, who was then passing by, observed to deponent, that man is fully committed, you can now speak to him. That, conversation took place between Stivers and deponent in relation to his, Stivers's situation. This deponent told Stivers, that he could not be concerned for him without a fee. Upon which, the said Stivers observed, that he expected to pay deponent his fee, and inquired how much it was. Deponent told him, that he should charge him, in that case, twenty-five dollars. Stivers then said, that Mr. Colgate had got all his money from him, a great deal more than he had ever received from a division of the property stolen, and that his nephew, in Pearl-Street, whose name deponent does not now recollect, had funds in his hands belonging to him, Stivers, and proposed to give this deponent, an order on said nephew for the sum of twenty-five dollars, the amount of the fee which he, said Stivers, had agreed to give this deponent to become his counsel, which order was drawn on the person, and delivered by the said Stivers, to the deponent. And this deponent further saith, that on calling on the nephew of the said Stivers, for the payment of the said order, he, deponent, was informed by the said nephew, that his uncle, Stivers, had drawn an order in favour of Mr. Colgate, covering all the funds which were, or should be in his hands, and that he had accepted the same. That this deponent requested the nephew to go up and see his uncle at the prison, which the nephew did, after some hesitation, when he related to his uncle the circumstance of his accepting the order in favour of Mr Colgate, and some, other conversation took place between Stivers

* See affidavit of Frederick Stivers.

and his nephew, which deponent does not now recollect, when his nephew left him. Stivers, then in conversation with deponent, censured the conduct of Mr. Colgate, saying, that he (Colgate) had got all his money from him, and had not performed his promise, which, said Stivers alleged to be, that if he, Stivers, would give up the whole of his money, and tell the whole truth in relation to the persons concerned with him in stealing from the said Colgate, that he (Colgate) would have him discharged, which the said Stivers alleged he had complied with, and that Colgate refused to let him out of prison, under the pretence, that one of the other persons concerned in the alleged felony, had disclosed more than he, said Stivers, had. That the said Stivers, while relating this story to deponent, burst into tears, and begged that deponent would assist him, and that he, Stivers, would put property into deponent's hands to secure him. That this deponent asked what kind of property it was, to which the said Stivers replied, that he had a watch and some furniture. This deponent observed to the said Stivers, that it had been customary for lawyers to receive property to secure fees, or in payment of fees; yet this deponent had avoided receiving property under these circumstances whenever he could, upon which Stivers exhibited great distress of mind, begging deponent to receive property as a security for this deponent's fee, and as soon as he got out he would redeem it, when he offered deponent an order on his wife for a silver watch, a small table, which the said Stivers said he had taken for rent, and which he said was not in use, and a single bedstead, which he also said was not in use. Deponent, from the story told him by the said Stivers, and knowing that he had been confined in the prison under examination for several days, together with the fact of his being fully committed, after his having made the disclosures, and delivered up his money, was lead to believe, that the said Stivers would be benefitted by counsel, as there had been evidently deception practised upon him in the neglect or refusal to discharge him, he, this deponent, did, thereupon, consent to take an order from said Stivers to secure his fee. That deponent, on calling at the house of the said Stivers, informed his wife of the order, and, at the same time, stated to her, that if the articles named in the order were of any use to her, or that she would suffer any inconvenience by deponents taking them, he, this deponent, would not take them. To which she replied, that they were of no use to the family, and that she would rather this deponent would take them than not. This deponent was informed, and which he verily believes to be true, that when it was discovered that when he was employed as counsel for the said Stivers, that then, and not till then, was the said Stivers released, which was then on giving bail to answer to the felony, on which he had been fully committed. That during the time the said Stivers was in custody in the bridewell, this deponent was informed by Mr. Nickles, the keeper of said prison, that there were some suggestions or complaints in the police office, and told deponent he had better go there and defend himself. Deponent immediately returned to the police office, and while there, in conversation with Josiah Hedden, one of the police magistrates, this deponent expostulated with the said Hedden on the impropriety of giving circulation to every petty slander, when this deponent was ready to explain any attack made upon him, the said Stivers came from the prison into the police office, when deponent remarked to the said Hedden, " there is the man himself," referring to the said Stivers, put any question to him you please ? Upon which the said Hedden commenced examining the said Stivers as to the truth of the suggestions made to him. (the said Hedden.) Upon finishing the said examination, the said Hedden expressed himself satisfied with the conduct of the deponent, and sent the said Stivers back to prison. This deponent then understood, to his utter astonishment, that the said Hedden had afterwards directed the clerk of the police to take the deposition of the said Stivers in relation to the same transaction, which deposition is annexed to the presentment found against this deponent, as deponent is informed, and believes. That this deponent has never been tendered his fee, which the said Stivers secured to be paid to him, but has permitted the said Stivers to take away the bedstead before mentioned, as he alleged he wanted to use the same. That said Stivers has since consulted with deponent as to the course to be pursued in recovering back the money taken from him by the said Colgate, suggesting, that he (said Stivers) could prove that that said money amounted to more than all the property stolen.

And this deponent has since understood from the said Stivers, that Colgate had given up part of the money or property taken from him the said Stivers. And this deponent further saith, that the annexed deposition made by the said Frederick Stivers was, before he swore to the same, twice distinctly read and explained to him, and that he perfectly understood the intent and meaning thereof. That this deponent has always been ready and willing to give up said property on the payment of his fee. And this deponent further saith, that the said Stivers, with others concerned in the said robbery, were indicted for a conspiracy to cheat the said Colgate; and the said Stivers, and others was about to be put upon his trial, when deponent expostulated with the public prosecutor, and succeeded in having the said Stivers's name stricken out of the clerk's minutes as one of the defendants, and made a witness in behalf of the people. That the said Davis, Burger and Milligan spoken of in the affidavit of the said Stivers, annexed to the said presentment, consulted with this deponent as their counsel. That this deponent has procured a pardon for the said Davis from the president of the United States, and attended to the business of the said Burger, who was imprisoned for an assault and battery, untill he was released. That this deponent had no other connection with either the said Davis, Burger or Milligan, than what necessarily arose from a discharge of his professional duty;

and this deponent doth further say, that the foregoing statement. according to the best of his reccollection and belief, is the truth, the whole truth, and nothing but the truth; and further the deponent saith not.

Geo. W. Niven.

Sworn before me, this first day of June, 1822. *F. A. Talmadge, Commissioner, &c.*

CITY OF NEW-YORK, SS.

George W. Niven being duly sworn, doth depose and say, that William Charley, in the deposition annexed to the presentment against this deponent, while in the bridewell of this city, on a charge of purchasing stolen goods, employed deponent as his counsel, in the ordinary way of business. The said William Charley was desirous of being bailed, and promised this deponent five dollars for his trouble, in endeavouring to procure bail for him. The said Charley said that he had no money, but that the police had taken from him a watch, which he would give deponent an order for, and did so. On deponents applying to the police with the said order for the watch, the police refused to deliver the same to this deponent, alleging, that there was reason to believe that it was stolen. This deponent did however exert himself to procure bail for the said Charley, but did not succeed, which deponent informed the said Charley of. The said Charley, told deponent, that if deponent would go on with his business, he the said Charley would endeavour to procure the five dollars in a few days; that a short time thereafter, the said Charley paid deponent the five dollars. That it is utterly untrue as is stated in the deposition of the said William Charley, that this deponent ever agreed or undertook to defend the cause of the said William Charley for five dollars only, but on the contrary, the said five dollars as first charged, was expressly understood to be as a compensation to deponent, for using his exertions to procure bail for the said Charley. That said Charley, upon said charge, was afterwards indicted, when he again applied to deponent for his aid, counsel, and advice, at which time deponent told the said Charley, that he must pay or secure deponent a fee before he would undertake as counsel to defend him under that indictment. The said Charley replied, that he was willing to give deponent his fee, but that he had no money or other means to secure deponent, except the watch spoken of in said Charley's deposition, which is the same watch shown to Peter Field, in the annexed deposition named.

That deponent agreed to take the risk of getting the said watch from the police, proceeded in the preparation of his defence, and succeeded in obtaining his acquittal before a jury, as appears by the certificate of the clerk hereunto annexed. That this deponent saw the said Charley after his acquittal, and in a conversation with him, said Charley expressed great gratitude for the services that deponent had rendered him, and told deponent that there were no services that he could render deponent, but what he would be always ready to do. That deponent **never saw the** said Charley afterwards, till he came to deponent's house, evidently from his conduct, in a state of intoxication, and **to the astonishment of deponent, he told deponent that he wanted his watch.** Deponent expostulated with him, and reminded him of what had previously transpired, and that the watch was not the said Charley's, that said Charley's conduct was abusive, so much so, that it disturbed deponents family, and deponent was compelled to order said Charley out of his house. And that all the statements contained in said Charley's deposition, imputing fraud or a want of good faith in deponent are utterly false.

George W. Niven.

Sworn to the 1st day of June, 1822, *before me F. A. Talmage, commissioner.*

The counsel then read a certificate of the acquittal of Charley, W. Niven being his counsel.

CITY OF NEW.YORK. SS.

Peter Field jun. of the said city, being duly affirmed, saith, that he is now and has for several years last past, been a manufacturer and vender of watches in this city. That he has examined a double cased silver watch shewn him by George W. Niven, and affirmant, considers the said watch, worth from ten to twelve dollars, and no more, and further affirmant saith not.

Peter Field, jun.

Affirmed before me the 31*st day of May* 1822. *Geo. Wilson. commissioner under the act of* 24*th March,* 1822.

CITY AND COUNTY OF NEW-YORK, SS.

George W. Niven, of said city, being duly sworn, doth depose and say, that Alexander Kerland, named in the deposition annexed to the presentment against deponent, was put upon his trial together with James Stewart, at the May sessions 1821, on the charge of passing counterfeit money, as by the clerk's certificate hereunto annexed appears ; and this deponent doth further say, that the said Alexander Kerland and James Stewart, since then were taken up in the house of Timothy Conner and Guy Fuller, and imprisoned in the Bridewell of this city, upon-the charge, as this deponent is informed and believes, of being concerned in dealing in counterfeit money ; that the said Stewart and Kerland were intimate acquaintances, and both employed this deponent, to defend them ; that this deponent after being employed, applied to the police, and used all his exertions to get the said Kerland liberated, and that no money being found upon him, he was continued in bridewell with the view, as this deponent understood, with the view of endeavouring of getting some information or complaint against him ; and that one or two other persons who were taken up in the same house at the same time, had offered to become witnesses in behalf of the people, and disclose the whole;

but as there was no direct testimony against the said Kerland, and after frequent applications made by this deponent in his behalf, he was discharged. That the said James Stewart, the friend of the said Kerland, was tried and convicted, and this deponent was his counsel; and that after the said Kerland was discharged, he frequently applied to this deponent in behalf of the said Stewart, begging of him to make use of all his exertions to have the said Stewart acquitted. and he, Kerland, would pay this deponent for his trouble, but which he has never done; that the said Kerland when he employed this deponent, which was in the ordinary way of business, gave this deponent an order on Peter M'Ardle for five dollars, leaving five dollars unpaid, and which he promised to pay when he got out. On deponents applying to M'Ardle he refused to pay the amount and took deponent to a person who was acquainted with Kerland in Ireland, but who informed deponent that he had assisted Kerland in his difficulties before when he was implicated with Stewart, and that he would have nothing more to do with him, and that he might get out as well as he could. Deponent returning and informing Kerland what his friends said, he, Kerland, offered to give this deponent a trunk of clothing for the said ten dollars, and then gave an order on Mc'Ardle for said trunk of clothing in whose possession it then was: that the trunk of clothing referred to in the deposition of Henry K. Niven is the same trunk of clothing received by deponent on the order of the said Kerland. That this deponent several times after he was liberated requested of him to come and take away said trunk, and pay the money, that he promised deponent to do so, and in the conversation previous to the last, which this deponent had with him, he told this deponent, that if he did not, he this deponent might sell them or do what he pleased with them; that after the time had elapsed in which he was to have redeemed them, deponent examined the trunk and found them of very small value, and he belives he gave two or three of the old worn garments, to poor people, and that after this, when the said Kerland came to demand the said trunk of clothing, this deponent was astonished at the demand after what had previously passed, and told him so, and that after the said Kerland went out of deponent's office, deponent told the person who came with Kerland, that he deponent had given away some of the things he believed, that he would see what were left, and as they were of little or no value, he might have them, upon which, he Kerland and his friend, went away together and never called again. And further this deponent saith not.

Geo. W. Niven.

Sworn this 1st day of June, 1822, before me,
F. A. Talmadge, Commissioner, &c.

To this was annexed the Clerk of the Sessions (Mr. Hatfield's) certificate of the acquittal of James Stewart and Alexander Kerland, on an indictment for having in their possession and passing a counterfeit note of the bank of New-York, scienter and that Kirland was used as a witness.

CITY OF NEW-YORK, ss.

George W. Niven, being duly sworn doth depose and say, that he has read copies of the depositions of Ellen Griffin, and Thomas M. Collins, as served upon him by order of this honourable court. That the said Ellen Griffin did employ this deponent while she was in the bridewell of this city, as her counsel. This deponent then understood, and believes, that the said Ellen Griffin was arrested by the said Thomas M. Collins, upon a charge of having robbed a person, whose name is unknown to deponent, of a considerable sum of money. That this deponent was in consultation frequently with said Ellen, on the said charge, and that during an investigation of the causes which led to her arrest, having had frequent conversations with the said Thomas M. Collins, this deponent was led to believe, that although the said money had been stolen, yet, that the said Thomas M. Collins had caused her to be arrested, more as a matter of speculation on his part, than for the ends of public justice. This deponent was informed, that the said Thomas M. Collins, after the arrest and imprisonment of said Ellen Griffin, had a direct agency in obtaining from the said Ellen a delivery of her property and effects, into the hands of the person from whom the money was alleged to have been stolen by the said Ellen Griffin. That this deponent understood the said person from whom the money was taken, was a respectable farmer from Long Island, who, not liking the idea of an exposition of the transactions attending the loss of his money, in open court, did succeed in negociating the matter through Thomas M. Collins, by which the felony was compounded, and for which, as deponent was informed by Thomas M. Collins, he, said Thomas M. Collins, received for his trouble five dollars. And this deponent further saith, that in the course of his practice in the criminal department of this city, he had formed an opinion and belief, that persons were frequently apprehended upon charges of felony, the matter compromised by restitution of the thing stolen on indemnity, and, then, as vagrants, committed to the penitentiary, whereby the prisoner is deprived of the right of trial by jury, in direct violation, as he conceived, of the constitution of the United States, the state of New-York, and the bill of rights. That the circumstances attending the compromise with Ellen Griffin, and her subsequent confinement as a vagrant in the penitentiary, was an additional instance in his mind of the illegality of such proceedings, and he, this deponent, was anxious to press the examination as to her guilt or innocence upon the charge for a felony before a jury, and with that view to prevent a compromise, as well as to indemnify this deponent for the trouble and expense which he might be put to as her counsel, he obtained from the said Ellen Griffin the power of attorney, which is hereunto annexed. That under, and by virtue of the said power, this deponent called on John Cornell, therein named, and demanded from him the delivery of the property of her, the said Ellen, when said Cornell informed deponent, that the property was not in his possession, but had, as deponent understood him to say, been delivered at the instance of said Collins, to a third person. And with a view to a further investigation, he, this deponent, caused a suit to be instituted in the name of said Ellen, against said Cornell. That after the said suit was commenced, the said Thomas M. Collins came to deponent, and told him, that he had obtained the property back, and if deponent would go with him to the place where the property was, it should be delivered, which was, accordingly, done. This deponent, thereupon, discontinued the suit, and paid the costs, and, also, one dollar and fifty cents to the said Collins, claimed by him for his agency and services, in obtaining back said property. That the allegations made by the said Thomas M Collins, first, that deponent claimed said articles as his own; secondly, that deponent said, " that she (Ellen) might do as she pleased, and go to hell," is utterly false. That on the said Thomas M. Collins claiming said property in the name of Ellen Griffin, this deponent showed the said property to him, and requested him to take it away. This deponent was unusually cautious at the time, supposing, that the said Thomas M. Collins was an emissary from the police, sent to entrap this deponent. The said Thomas M. Collins, instead of taking said property, hesitated, and evidently seemed disappointed at the anxiety exhibited by the deponent, that he should take the property away. And replied to deponent's request, that he would see said Ellen, and call upon deponent the next morning, which the said Thomas M. Collins did not do. That the said Ellen Griffin, as this deponent has been informed by the said Thomas M. Collins, is a common prostitute at Corleas Hook. That this deponent never did enter into any stipulation or condition with the said Ellen Griffin, that he would get her released for any sum of money, but that his employment as counsel was done in the ordinary way, and subject to the usual contingencies governing such an employment. That deponent rendered her all the services which he could, under the circumstances of the case That this deponent, when the said Ellen Griffin called upon him, was under an impression, that Mrs. Niven had given away the hat; but, upon subsequent inquiry, he finds, that in relation to that fact, he was mistaken. Deponent considers the whole of said property mere trash, not worth to exceed, in the whole, the sum of ten dollars.

George W. Niven.

Sworn before me, this 22d of June, 1822. *John L. Broome, Clerk.*

·Annexed was a printed power of attorney from Ellen Griffin to George W. Niven, counsellor at law, to recover to his use, all, &c. in the usual form.

CITY OF NEW YORK, SS.

Betsey Garland of the City of New-York, being duly sworn, saith that she has heard read to her the affidavit of Thomas M. Collins, and also the affidavit of Ellen Griffin, and this deponent further saith, that she was present and heard what passed in a conversation between George W. Niven, and the said Thomas M. Collins. Mr. Niven did not at any time during said conversation, allege or say the said articles were his, or any words to that effect. No such expression was used as is stated in the affidavit of Collins, " that she (Ellen) might do as she pleased and go to h—l," Collins told Mr. Niven he came to get the things, and would pay five dollars. Mr. Niven told him he might take them, and showed Collins the articles. Collins seemed then to hesitate and finally concluded that he would again see the girl, and call again the next morning, which he did not do. During all the conversation, Mr. Niven appeared anxious that Collins should take the things away, and this deponent further saith, that she has at the request of Mr. Niven, carefully examined the said articles. The hat is riped apart, and from her examination all the articles in her opinion is not worth at most over ten dollars, deponent has lived in the family of Mr. Niven over eight months, and the said trunk and articles has remained as they were in the trunk undisturbed, and this deponent further saith, that Mrs. Niven some months since, did give away a black leghorn bonnet to a little girl in the country, and further deponent saith not.

her
Betsey ⋈ Garland.
mark

Sworn before me this 22d of June 1822. Wm. Lowerie commissioner under act of March, 1818.

The two nisi prius records of G. W. Niven's acquittal at the June sittings, 1820, were then produced. These indictments, Mr Anthon observed, set forth the whole of the matters now charged in the affidavit of Latimer. On both of them he was tried, and acquitted at the sittings of the Supreme Court. And upon examining one of these records, the only witness examined for the prosecution was this Thomas Latimer, and the jury not believing in the truth of what he swore, acquitted Mr. Niven.

Mr. Maxwell. I understood it never went to the jury.

Mr. Anthon. I state it from my own knowledge. Mr. Maxwell was not concerned. Mr. Van Wyck was then attorney for the district. Mr. Latimer was a witness, and made himself so ridiculous, that the jury disregarded all he said, and acquitted the defendant.

In the other case, there were a number of witnesses and Latimer, Baker and Kissam, were examined and the jury say that defendant is not guilty.

I should like now added the counsel to be favored with the opinion of the Court, whether this record is not conclusive, and, of course, whether it is of any use to trouble the court with affidavits to deny a charge which stands disproved by record; and I should request the opinion of the whole court upon this question.

First Judge. The court think it not for them to interfere, but leave the party to show such cause as he thinks, or is advised is sufficient, and to go on till he thinks he has shown enough cause.

Mr. Anthon. Then we must pray leave to introduce a host of affidavits, if the record of acquittal is not held sufficient to protect us He again asked for the opinion of the whole court.

First Judge. I have consulted all the judges, and the opinion I have given is that of the whole court.

Mr. Anthon. We must, then, demand more time, we thought the record of acquittal was the highest of all evidence, and not to be controverted.

Mr Price. This is the first case of the kind, that has ever occurred, and that we might, therefore, even ask for the advice and directions of the court, as to the form and methods of the proceedings.

Mr. Maxwell said the case was not without precedent, and referred to the case of the King against Southerton, an attorney, 6 East, 142, where the judgment was arrested, and the defendant discharged; yet the Chief Justice said, that enough appeared to satisfy them, that he was an improper person to remain as an attorney upon the rolls of the court, and a rule was made to show cause why he should not be struck off, which the defendant yielded to, and his name was accordingly struck off, his counsel admitting that he could not resist it.

Mr. Anthon. As Mr. Justice Yates, who tried the indictment, did not think proper to take any such step, the time is of course gone by. And the record, we think, should now be conclusive evidence, that the party is not guilty. But if it be not so, we have witnesses in every quarter, some even in England, and we cannot tell how long it may be before we can lay their affidavits before the court.

General Bogardus. There is another distinction; that case of Southerton was not the case of an indictable offence, but this is. And the party's *acquittal* here, was upon the merits. There the party was convicted upon the merits, and the judgment was arrested on mere technical grounds.

First Judge. If this case should seem to turn upon that point, we should give time to get the affidavits in explanation, and take the record of acquittal as *prima facie* evidence in favour of the defendant.

Mr. Anthon then read the following affidavit of H. K. Niven, touching the affidavit of Charley, to show. that Stivers was fully apprized of the contents of his second affidavit.

CITY AND COUNTY OF NEW-YORK, SS.

Henry K. Niven, now about to leave the said city, being duly sworn, saith, that he was present sometime in the latter part of the months of September, or the first of October last, at a conversation which took place between George W. Niven, Esq., and two persons, one of whom was named William Charley, and the other name not mentioned, but who appeared as the friend of Charley, and who said to George W. Niven, Esq., you have now received the watch of Charley, and five dollars, will you exert yourself to have him acquitted : Mr. Niven said he would. Charley and his friend appeared pleased upon which Mr. Niven left them. And deponent further saith, that the annexed affidavit made by Frederick Stivers was read to said Stivers twice, slow and distinct, so that he Stivers perfectly understood the contents of the same before the said Stivers swore to the same before judge Irving ; and the said Stivers offered to make the affidavit before the same was drawn. And this deponent further saith, that the trunk of clothes spoken of as having been got from Alexander Kerland, he deponent took an inventory, and valued, and the whole amount including the trunk was not worth over ten dollars.

Henry K. Niven.

Sworn before me this 9*th day of March,* 1822. *Nathan B Graham, commissioner.*

He also read a certificate of three of the grand jurors, that there was no other evidence before them, than the three affidavits that accompanied their presentment, which was in these words.

New-York, May, 31st 1822.

We the undersigned, grand jurors, when the presentment was found against George W. Niven, do certify *first*, that the presentment was found by the jury against Mr. Niven on the *ex parte* evidence of the people. *Secondly,* that to our best recollection and belief, there were but *three* depositions before us, two of whom were or had been charged with felonies. That there was no other evidence before us against Mr. Niven on which the presentment was ordered.

S. Gould.
Kinloch Stuart.
John M'Clure.

Also the affidavit of George W. Niven, showing the necessity of further time.

NEW-YORK, COMMON PLEAS,

CITY AND COUNTY OF NEW-YORK,

George W. Niven, being duly sworn, saith, that upon examination of the depositions, copies of which have been served on this deponent since the last term of this court, he finds them abounding with facts, which are discoloured and untrue, and which cannot be explained or corrected by this deponent without reference to persons whom this deponent has not been able to see, and without statements of this deponent and others necessarily so voluminous as to require more time than has been given, for the purpose of explanation to this deponent, and this deponent further saith. that he is advised by counsel, that further time is absolutely necessary for the purposes above referred to.

George W. Niven.

Sworn before me, this 22*d day of June,* 1822. *R. Riker.*

Mr. *Maxwell* thought these to be frivolous grounds of delay. What were the affidavits to be answered by further and other testimony? That of Couheuhoven touching conversations between those two persons, and facts of which no other person could have any knowledge; and those of Collins and Shoemaker.

Mr. *Niven* denied all intention of seeking to screen himself from inquiry, or interposing any useless delay. He stated, that his brother H. K. Niven, was now employed in an agency in the back part of Pennsylvania. He said he had been traced back through ten years of his life, and only wanted to make his depositions with correctness, and not to let the refutation of these charges rest entirely upon his own evidence. These were not shallow or frivolous pretences, but considerations of vital importance to his family, and reputation. The delay was at his own pain, it was he that remained on the rack, tortured by feelings which those gentlemen knew nothing of. He was willing, however, to bear the burthen, and to suffer those feelings, to remain planted in the bosom of himself, and of his family, in order that his exculpation might be complete. Whatever the district attorney might think or say, nine tenths of the community would consider it a harsh measure to press against one of his own profession, what would deprive him of his means of justification. If he called upon individuals in this city, they would tell him they were afraid of offending the police. If they compel us, they say, we must testify. If I go to the first judge, and show him subpœnas granted by Mr. Hedden to witnesses, to come and testify against me, he cannot give me subpœnas to bring witnesses from the bear market, and compel them to come on my behalf. In the case of Mr. Latimer's prosecution, there was justice, and sixty-three witnesses were present to testify against him.

(Here Mr. Niven was proceeding in terms of recrimination against the opposite counsel, when the court interposed, and he continued.)

The court do not know my feelings, but this city has known my ancestors; my grandfather lived in this city, and in this city he descended with honour to the grave. I mean to do the same. If I have committed any errors, they are not wilful or intentional. And, however fastidious that gentleman may be, I pledge myself to his refutation. I owe it to myself, to my wife, my two children, and to Robert Johnson, that my name shall not be long disgraced. I am willing to resign my station on the earth, but I must first do that duty to myself and my family. Mr Niven then made some observations on the transactions which he would explain in due time, being prepared with a chain of circumstances which would confute the whole of the charges. He complained of the hardship of his position, which affected his feelings so much that he could not lie still upon his pillow, but was driven to have recourse to anodynes to procure a small part of that rest which God had been pleased to bestow upon his his creatures as their solace and restorer. He was willing that the inquiry should go back to his cradle, though the commonest culprit can avail himself of statute limitations to penalties and prosecutions. He was willing his children should be taken to the almshouse, but not that their father should be disgraced.

General Bogardus thought the expressions of the district attorney rather unkind, and hoped the court would consider this as an ordinary application for time growing out of the necessity of the case, some of the charges went back five years, some three, some two. Affidavits touching transactions which took place five years ago, were served but the week before the last; and though Mr. Niven has answered some of them, we are of opinion, that with a little more time, he will answer them more fully. The party who carries on the prosecution, has the power of the police, which is, in this city, very great. The witnesses are vagabonds and vagrants, over whom the justices have entire control. I have seen two citations to come and appear and testify. Here he read a subpœna issued from the police office in the usual printed form, to a witness to come and testify in a matter between the people and G. W. Niven. Mr. Niven has no such power, and until the people get over their fears of the police, he cannot lay before this court his evidence. And this being a matter which regards the honour and dignity of this court, as well as his own safety, we only ask till the next court, when we shall, if possible, be fully prepared to answer the affidavits of Davenport, Shoemaker, and Couhenhoven

First Judge. We consider this as a very important cause, as regards the community, the court, the party, and the profession. We think there should be time for a thorough investigation of the conduct of a member of this bar so seriously circumstanced. We will, therefore, adjourn till the first Saturday in the next term.

Mr. Niven said he would have to correspond with one person in the back parts of Pennsylvania, and the time allowed would be short enough.

Mr. Maxwell. If a thorough investigation is the object, I shall request to have some other affidavits read, containing charges of equal turpitude with those before the court, and we now offer those further affidavits, which he will have full time to answer.

Mr. Price. The three affidavits sent by the Supreme Court, to be examined into in this court, is all that we suppose we have to answer.

First Judge. We shall call upon the party to exculpate himself from the charges now before us, and shall not carry our present inquiry beyond those.

Mr. Niven complained of the newspaper publications which would prevent people from doing any business with him.

First Judge. We have already expressed an opinion, that there ought to be no more of these publications till the examination be concluded.

July 20th, 1822.

This day the following affidavits and documents were read on the part of Mr. Niven.

CITY AND COUNTY OF NEW-YORK, SS.

George W. Niven, being duly sworn, doth depose and say : that at the time of being served with the deposition of John J. Shoemaker, he had no recollection whatever of the name. That on applying at 19 Murray-Street, to inquire concerning him, he found said Shoemaker was not a merchant as he represents himself, but a distressed object of charity, who had lived a part of the last winter at the bounty of Walter F. Osgood, Esq. That upon reflection as to the circumstances attending the case of George Peers, this deponent remembers having seen said Shoemaker, who was to have been bail of said Peers, who was committed to bridewell, upon a charge of stealing a coat. That this deponent took little interest in said case, until said Shoemaker applied to this deponent in Warren-Street, and represented that he was a freeholder holding property in the upper part of the City, and lived in Dey-Street, between Greenwich and Washington-Street, and wished to become the bail of said Peers ; at the same time asking deponent the effect of being security for him, in the event of his running away, to which deponent answered according to the best of his knowledge and belief, if Peers runs away, you will have to pay the amount of your recognizance, unless you can get it remitted by the Court of Exchequer. That supposing from the professions of said Shoemaker, that he was competent security, this deponent inquired for him in Dey-Street, where he had been directed, but could find no such person as Shoemaker, or any person who knew him, and there the matter terminated.

That this deponent is confident, that no such conversation passed as Shoemaker has related. That the suggestion as to Peers running away, and the subsequent request to be silent about it, is so remarkable, that deponent could not have forgotten it, had such a thing occurred, and having no recollection of it, this deponent therefore contends according to the best of his knowledge and belief, that the same is utterly false, and further deponent saith not.

George W. Niven.

Sworn this 20*th day of July*, 1822, *before me.* J. L. Broome, *clerk.*

CITY AND COUNTY OF NEW-YORK, SS.

Walter F. Osgood, of the said City being duly sworn, doth depose and say, that he this deponent keeps his office at No. 19 Murray-Street, that he has known John J. Shoemaker, since the 24th of October, 1820, that he became acquainted with his indigent circumstances shortly after the first acquaintance, that the beginning of last winter said Shoemaker was in the habit occasionally of frequenting this deponents office, who admitted him to the same, and to warm himself near deponents fire, that deponent was always in the habit for the last twelve months of insisting on his clerks sleeping in his office, and the said Shoemaker advancing from one step to another, finally was in the habit of sleeping also in deponents office, which circumstance was not made known to deponent by his clerk for some time, deponent felt displeased at it, but from the inclemency of the weather, and the information deponent had received of the respectability of said Shoemaker's family, he allowed the same. The general reputation of said Shoemaker as to veracity and truth is bad, and from circumstances which are known to this deponent, he should not feel inclined to believe him under oath. Part of the time said Shoemaker was in the habit of sleeping in deponents office, it was on the floor, said Shoemaker was in the habit of doing little menial errants, for which deponent occasionally supplied him with victuals and money out of humanity. Said Shoemaker has represented himself at different times not only to this deponent, but other individuals as having been a merchant, a sea captain, a major in the United States army, a lawyer, an agent for the United States, a broker, a keeper of an intelligence office, and of some other professions which this deponent at present does not recollect, so as to be able to specify and state the same.

W. F. Osgood.

Sworn to this 19th day of July, 1822, before me. R. Riker.

CITY AND COUNTY OF NEW-YORK, SS.

Asa Holden of the said city, deposes and says, that he is well acquainted with John J. Shoemaker, that the said Shoemakers character as to veracity and truth is bad, and that he has heard said Shoemaker tell the most improbable stories, and that he would not believe him under oath.

Asa Holden.

Sworn to this 19th day of July, 1822, before me. R. Riker.

CITY AND COUNTY OF NEW-YORK, SS.

George W. Niven, in answer to the deposition of Edward Couhenhoven, of the county of Westchester, being duly sworn, doth depose and say, that as appears by an entry in the register of this deponent, and which he believes to be correct, he received from the said Edward Couhenhoven, in said deposition, mentioned the account hereunto annexed, marked A, against one Jacob Acker, Jun. and upon which account this deponent commenced a suit in the Mayor's Court of the city of New-York, by the direction of said Couhenhoven, and which suit was prosecuted, as appears by the certificate of John L. Broome, Esq. hereunto annexed, marked G. That on the sixth day of January, 1817, as appears endorsed on document B, after the declaration had been filed in said cause, he received from the said Edward Couhenhoven, by mail, the annexed letter, marked B, requesting him to stop all further proceedings, and to send to the said Couhenhoven his bill of costs. That he, this deponent, made out a bill of costs, which is hereunto annexed, marked E, amounting to sixteen dollars twenty-four and an half cents, which was not paid, and in relation to which suit, he, subsequently, to wit, on the sixth of June in said year, received the order hereunto annexed, marked D, requesting him to proceed to judgment in said suit, though, afterwards, upon the arrival in town of said Couhenhoven, deponent was informed, that the said suit was arranged, or about to be so, between the parties.

And this deponent further saith, that in the month of January, 1817, he was employed by the said Edward Couhenhoven or his bail, to defend a suit brought against him by one Peter Sherwood, upon which occasion, Jackson Haines, of the third ward, of the city of New-York, grocer, (now deceased,) was the bail for the said Couhenhoven, notice of which bail being filed, was given by this deponent to Josiah Hedden, Esq. the attorney for the said Sherwood, though, afterwards, James Smith, Esq. appearing to conduct the said defence, it was relinquished by this deponent, at the request of the said Couhenhoven, and the bill of costs hereunto annexed, marked F, was charged to the said Edward Couhenhoven.

And this deponent further saith, that he was, afterwards, employed by the said Edward Couhenhoven to defend a suit, brought against him in the Marine Court of the city of New-York, wherein Thomas Stevens was the plaintiff, the particulars of which are set forth in the annexed certificate, marked C, and which said suit is the one referred to in the deposition of said Couhenhoven. That this deponent is not confident as to the actual amount of money deposited in his hands upon being the security; but as the amount of the verdict was twenty-five dollars one cent, and the amount of the claim was only thirty-three dollars, he does not think the sum deposited amounted to forty dollars, and, in fact, instead of the sum of money claimed, as stated by the said Couhenhoven, being thirty-seven dollars and some cents, it was only thirty-three dollars, as appears by the certificate before referred to. And deponent further saith, that he became such surety at the solicitation of said Couhenhoven, and that, at the time of becoming so, no judgment was rendered, and, consequently, no means of ascertaining how much money would cover the same; nor is it probable, that the money could have been received by the court, they not knowing the sum to be paid; at all events, however, this deponent remembers, that he became surety upon the express promise of said Couhenhoven to deposit in his hands enough to cover said judgment; that, afterwards, at this deponent's office, a certain sum of money was deposited in his hands, but how much exactly, deponent does not now recollect, at all events, however, no money, according to the best of this deponent's knowledge and belief, was theretofore received from the said Couhenhoven as a fee, or otherwise, and deponent further saith, that he has no recollection of making use of the expression which is alleged to have been made by him, and that after the rendering of said judgment, and after the term had expired for defendant to pay in consequence of the plaintiff being a non resident, no steps were immediately taken upon said judgment.

And this deponent further saith, that after waiting sometime he was called upon as the surety for the said Couhenhoven, to pay the amount of the said judgment, rendered against him in the Marine Court; that, waiting to see said Couhenhoven, in order to have their accounts liquidated, he was prosecuted in the Mayor's Court of the city of New-York, by Benjamin Tucker, Esq. (now deceased,) on behalf of said Thomas Stevens, the plaintiff in the Marine Court, which this deponent defended, and in which suit this deponent obtained a judgment, as appears by the certificate of John L. Broome, Esq. hereunto annexed, marked H, and that, afterwards, the said Couhenhoven promised to pay to this deponent the amount of his bill of costs hereunto annexed, marked I ; but this deponent has never received the same, or any money whatever from said Couhenhoven, according to the best of his knowledge and belief, beyond the sum of money so given as aforesaid to this deponent, in his office, according to the best of his knowledge and belief, after he became such security as aforesaid, in the Marine Court. That this deponent, and the said Couhenhoven had an explanation in relation to this business, after the judgment was obtained by this deponent in the Mayor's Court, as last spoken of, and upon that occasion the said Couhenhoven expressed himself perfectly satisfied, and promised to pay the bill of costs attending the defence of the same.

That as to the allegation of said Couhenhoven, that this deponent "had no claim or demand whatever to his knowledge on said money, or any part thereof." This deponent says it is utterly false, and from all the circumstances must have been known to be so by the said Couhenhoven unless he has very singularly forgotten the circumstances which have been detailed by this deponent.

And this deponent further saith, that according to the best of his knowledge and belief, at the time above referred to of an explanation between this deponent and said Couhenhoven in relation to their accounts, and before said Couenhoven expressed himself satisfied therewith, this deponent offered to submit the said accounts with said Couhenhoven to any tribunal by joining issue, and letting them determine the same, but this offer was declined by said Couhenhoven, and he expressed himself satisfied as aforesaid, and further this deponent saith not. Geo. W. Niven.

Sworn this 20th day July, 1822, before me, Jno. L. Broome, Clk.

Annexed was the following statement.

Couhenhoven vs. Acker,	$10 24 1-2
Couhenhoven ads. Sherwood,	5
Couhenhoven ads. Stevens,	10
Niven ads. Stevens,	14 62
	45 86 1-2

Postage at various times besides advice as counsel.

Annexed also to this deposition were the exhibits referred to the account against Acker on which Couhenhoven's suit was founded. A letter form Couhenhoven to G. W. Niven, dated Tarrytown, Jan. 2, 1817, apprising Mr. Niven that he had agreed to leave the case against Acker to arbitration, and directing him to stop all further proceedings therein. An exemplification of the judgment in the case of Stevens vs Couhenhoven, under the seal of the marine court, shewing the nature of the demand, and the amount of the judgment, and also that Mr. Niven was security for debt and costs. a direction from Edward Couhenhoven, to Geo. W. Nevin, as his attorney in the suit against Acker to proceed to judgment notwithstanding any order theretofore to the contrary. A bill of costs in the suit of Couhenhoven vs Acker, containing in detail the taxable items, amounting to $16 24 1-2. A like bill in the case of Couhenhoven vs. Peter Sherwood, amounting to $5. The like in the case of G. W. Niven vs. Stevens amouning to $14 62. A certificate from Jno. L. Broome clk. of the Common Pleas, that the capias in the suit of Couhenhoven vs. Acker was returned *cepi corpus* in December term, 1818, and that the common rules had been entered therein, and the declaration filed. And also a certificate from the said clerk in the case of Stevens vs. Geo. W. Niven, *gent. one* &c. that the bail piece in that cause was filed in October term 1817, that the defendant in person demurred, and that in November term following the defendant entered a rule for payment.

CITY AND COUNTY OF NEW-YORK, SS.

George W. Niven of said city, being duly sworn, doth depose and say, that at the solicitation and request of John Davenport, a butcher in the Washington Market, in April term, 1818, he commenced a suit against Samuel Bronson a drover, from Orange county. That the question involved in said cause, was an intricate one, and depended upon points of law which occupied the time of this deponent in research and legal application beyond what he had at first, reason to anticipate. That the said suit was prosecuted to judgment, and the verdict rendered was sixty-five dollars; which together with the costs, made the judgment amount to 90 dollars and 64 cents, which was entered upon on the 28th of July, 1818, as appears by the entries in this deponents register, which are no doubt correct. That the said Bronson was arrested by a special deputation from the sheriff, and after the completion of the judgment, a Mr. Fountain was with the necessary documents empowered by the said Davenport, to recover the amount of said judgment from the defendant, who resided in Orange county as aforesaid. That the said Fountain proceeded to collect the same, and accounted for the amount of said judgment *including the costs* to said John Davenport, not one cent of which was ever received by this deponent.

That considering the importance of said cause to the butchers generally, and the anxiousness with which said Davenport appeared to press it, and taking into consideration also, that the suit was brought to establish a principle, which though doubtful, had long been contended for by the butchers, and repelled by the drovers, this deponent was compelled to use uncommon diligence in his research as well as in preparing said cause for trial; for which this deponent charged the said Davenport a fee of twenty-five dollars, which at the time he did not consider unreasonable, and which the butchers friendly to said Davenport, then and since, have expressed as being very moderate.

That during the time said suit was pending, this deponent dealt with said Devenport as a butcher, and not knowing to the contrary, presumes the account as charged to this deponent to be correct.

And this deponent further saith, that he was also consulted frequently and repeatedly by said Davenport, in relation to some lands in the western part of this state, which were then or about to be a subject of litigation, and that this deponent in his professional capacity, counselled and advised the said Davenport in relation thereto; for which he this deponent justly considers himself entitled to compensation; but that for this as well as his counsel fee, and the costs in the suit against Bronson he never received to the best of his recollection and belief one cent. That some considerable time after this, but exactly how long or when, this deponent does not now recollect. Mr. Williamson placed in his hands by the order of Daniel Beadle of West-Chester county, an account in favour of said Beadle against said Davenport for collection, which this deponent presented, and requested payment. That this deponent received repeated assurances from time to time, that the same should be paid, and not wanting to prosecute one who had formerly been his client, this deponent indulged him until he discovered that he had no other alternative remaining, but the commencement of a suit. This deponent threatened to do so, when said Davenport pledged himself most sacredly to meet the demand by the time, that in the ordinary course of law he would be compelled to do so. That during all this time there was no pretence, that this deponent owed said Davenport any thing. That the time fixed upon as last before stated for the payment of said claim came round, and was yet unpaid, when for the first time said Davenport affected to have an account against this deponent beyond the amount of this deponents account for professional services. That he did, as represented by said Davenport ask him to make out his account, and did also say, that he did not think he owed said Davenport any thing. That he thought at the time the allegation of said Davenport, that deponent was indebted to him, was a mere pretence to defer the payment of Beadles claim, and an attempt to shuffle rid of it. Whereupon as this deponent was in duty bound, he commenced a suit in the Marine Court, and recovered a judgment for the amount; but by reason of the repeated and long continued indulgence granted to him by this deponent, the said Davenport became a bankrupt, went upon the limits, and thus defeated Mr. Beadle of his just and equitable claim, which had it been pressed, when first put into this deponents hands, or within a reasonable time thereafter, would no doubt have been paid.

And this deponent further saith, that the said John Davenport produced his account against this deponent, amounting probably to the sum specified in his deposition as an offset ; to which, this deponent produced (as he conceives he had a right to do) his account against Davenport, wherein he charged his taxable costs as an attorney in the suit of Davenport v. Bronson, and his counsel fee in that case, as well as a reasonable compensation for the advice given as counsel in relation to the western lands, a suit about which, as deponent understood, was then pending. That said account of this deponent was not trumped up merely to cover the amount of Davenport's bill, but was fairly, in justice and equity, what this deponent thought himself entitled to.

And this deponent further saith, that said Davenport, as this deponent conceives, through spite and irritation, brought a suit against this deponent in the Marine Court, upon his account, and this deponent not being allowed to set off counsel fees, but merely taxable costs as an attorney, the result was, a verdict was had against this deponent, as said Davenport, in his deposition, represents, for somewhere about twenty-five or six dollars, which this deponent has since paid.

That after the commencement of said suit against this deponent, feeling conscious of the correctness of his off-set, in good faith, though aware that, in all probability, a court of law would not allow it, being counsel fees, this deponent proposed to submit the reasonableness of it to Mr. M'Donald, who was then the attorney of said Davenport. That said Davenport at first consented, and although confined on the limits at the suit of Beadle as before stated, agreed to acompany this deponent to M'Donald's office ; that this was the true and only reason why said Davenport went with deponent off the limits, and was not the result of any trap or *insidious* contrivance to decoy him off as said Davenport has wrongfully and unjustly insinuated. That said Davenport, as this deponent has been informed and believes, was in the habit of breaking the limits, and the brother of this deponent had been for some days previous to that, endeavouring to fix the bail : but this deponent solemnly avers, that he did not know at the time where his brother was, or upon what errand he was engaged if out of the office, but concluded that he was at the office where deponent left him. That his brother according to the best of his knowledge and belief, was not with him in the market that morning, and that in relation to that fact, said Davenport, deponent believes, is mistaken. That this deponent did, it is true, go up Dey Street, and, notwithstanding the opinion of said Davenport to the contrary, his going up said street was not done to lead Davenport out of the way, to detain him an unnecessary time off the limits, or in any way to facilitate proceedings against him, or his sureties, for being off, and that the expression which this deponent is alleged to have made, that he had laid a plan to get or catch him off the limits must be somewhat exagerated, as he does not recollect precisely what passed in the presence of Mr. Jennings, but he feels confident that as he laid no plan to get Davenport off, he never could have used an expression signifying that he did.

The suit for the escape was tried, and it is true a verdict was rendered for the defendant, upon the principle as this deponent understood, that this deponent was an agent acting in the place and stead of the principal, that Davenport being in his company, was presumed to be in the company of the principal, and therefore the escape (if any) was inferred to be done by his assent and approbation.

And this deponent further saith, that upon the trial of said cause in the Marine Court, the brother of this deponent was called and examined as a witness for the defence, that according to the best of this deponents recollection and belief, he testified that there was no arrangement or understanding between him and this deponent to entrap said Davenport off the limits. That he had no knowledge whatever of any suit pending between this deponent and said Davenport: That this deponent left him in deponents office, and that he knew nothing of deponents intention of going to the market that morning. That he was not in company with this deponent in the Washington-Market that day, and that the proceedings were the result of his own volition and not preconcert or contrivance with this deponent.

And this deponent further saith, that these occurences took place during the pendency of Goodwin's trial, that this deponents brother was desirous of hearing the same as well as this deponent, and that he this deponent left his brother in the office while he went to see said Davenport for the purpose of getting the amount of this deponents account against him, referred to Mr. M'Donald, or in the event of being unsuccessful in that. to procure an adjournment of said cause, to enable him to be present at Goodwins trial, and that the first information which this deponent had of a suit for the escape of said Davenport, was derived from his brother and the officer whom they met in the street, and which was a surprize to this deponent, and further this deponent saith not.

George W. Niven.

Sworn this 20th day of July, 1822, before me.   J. L. Broome, clerk.

SUSQUEHANNAH COUNTY SS.

Henry K. Niven of the town of Gibson, Susquehanna county Pa. being duly sworn, saith, that in or about the month of March eighteen hundred and twenty, as near as this deponent can now recollect, he was on a visit to his brother George W. Niven Esq. in the city of New-York, and while there, his brother stated to deponent that one John Davenport, a butcher in the Washington-market, was then on the limits for a debt which the said Davenport, had when he was able, pleged his honor to pay, if he was not sued at such time as it could by a course of law be collected, that more than the time given had elapsed, and that instead of paying the claim, he had put his property out of his hands and went on the limits. This deponent considering the conduct of the said Davenport so dishonest and dishonourable, did consent to watch him as it was then believed that he was daily in the habit of going off the limits. And this deponent further saith that on the morning of the day Goodwin's trial was summed up, the said George told deponent that he had some business to do, and that he would return to the office and go with deponent to court, and endeavour to procure a seat for deponent, where he deponent could hear the council, and the said George went out from the office. Deponent remained for some time after in the office, and went down the street towards the market, and while walking carelessly down the street, deponent saw the said Davenport going towards Dey-street over the limits, upon which deponent went and had process issued against the said Davenport and his bail ; and this deponent further saith, that he had for several days occasionally watched the said Davenport before the process was issued. That deponent was not to his best reccollection and belief in the market the morning the process was issued, nor did he know that there was a suit pending between the said Davenport and the said George in court, nor did he know that the said George went from his office to the market until he accidentally saw him and Davenport going towards Dey-street, nor does this deponent recollect or believe that any conversation in relation to the said Davenport's being on the limits, or any thing on that subject was spoken of, or alluded to, between the said George and deponent on that morning ; and this deponent further saith, that the circumstances which took place that morning, so far as deponent knows, or believes, was not the result of concert or management, but altogether the result of accident, and further this deponent saith not.

Henry K. Niven.

Sworn before me, this 17th day of July, 1822. Joseph Washburn, Justice of the Police.

CITY OF NEW-YORK, SS.

Griffin Williamson, of the town of Poughkeepsie, being duly affirmed, says, that a ballance of thirty-five dollars and thirty-three cents, was due from John Davenport, butcher, in the Washington Market, to David Beadle of West Chester county ; affirmant called on the said Davenport frequently, and after repeated promises from the said Davenport to pay the same, none of which was performed, affirmant put the same, by order of Beadle, in the hands of George W. Niven, for collection, with a discretion on his part in the collection of the same, and further affirmant saith not.

G. Williamson.

Affirmed before me, this 12th of June, 1822. E. M'Garaghan.

CITY OF NEW-YORK, SS.

Jacob Aimes, and John Brewer, of the said city, butchers, standing in Washington Market, being severally duly sworn, depose and say, that the suit brought by John Davenport, also a butcher in said market, against a drover from Orange County, by the name of Brunson, for damages in refusing to deliver cattle according to agreement, was commenced for the sole purpose, and avowed object, of deciding a question which had produced considerable contention between the butchers and drovers, in this, that the drovers would agree to sell to one butcher, while they would speculate on the market, and if they could induce any other to give more than agreed upon with the first, would then sell to another.

The butchers, considering this conduct on the part of some of the drovers, an imposition upon them, determined to put the matter at rest by a suit at law, and, by common consent, it was concluded to employ George W. Niven, Esq. as the attorney and counsel for that purpose, and who was, accordingly, spoken to in the Washington Market upon that subject; who suggested, at the time, the uncertainty of a recovery by reason of a technical point of law, in relation to the delivery. And these deponents severally further say, that the said Davenport, at that time, disclaimed all intention of profiting by any recovery resulting from said suit, his professed object being, as was declared, to prevent a recurrence of the evil complained of, by establishing a precedent in a court of law And it was under these circumstances, that Mr. Niven was directed to go on and prosecute the suit.

And these deponents further severally say, that they were subpœnaed, and did attend the trial of said cause, and that George W. Niven, Esq. appeared, and conducted the same as the counsel for said Davenport.

And these deponents further severally say, that they were present at the conversation which took place in the market between the said Davenport and Mr. Niven, on the subject of their accounts, and that there was not, to either of their recollection or belief, any mention made of lands in Cincinnati, but there was as to lands in the western part of this state, in relation to which Mr. Niven said Mr. Davenport had consulted with him, and was indebted to him for his opinion as counsel.

And these deponents further severally say that they have heard said Davenport frequently speak of a law suit he had, or was about to have, in relation to lands in the western part of this state, and they saw Mr. Niven and said Davenport, frequently in private conversation, which they were led, at the time, and which they now believe related to that subject.

And these deponents further severally say, that from all the circumstances connected with the suit of Davenport against Brunson, the charge made by Mr. Niven, of twenty-five dollars, as a counsel fee in that case, is, in their opinion, reasonable and just, and ought to have been allowed to him by said Davenport, and further these deponents severally say not.

Jacob Aims.
John Brewer.

Sworn severally before me, this 16*th day of July,* 1822. *Cornelius Roosa, a Commissioner, &c.*

CITY OF NEW YORK, SS.

John Cornell, of the city of New-York, being duly sworn, doth depose and say, that he previously to the first of May last, kept a grocery store in Grand-Street. That he has a perfect recollection of a bonnet having been left at his store by Ellen Griffin. That Thomas M. Collins and a certain person whose name is unknown, but was represented by Collins as a farmer from Long Island, and was said to be a person from whom the said Ellen had stolen some money, came to this deponents store, and the said Collins then delivered to him the bonnet belonging to said Ellen. That at the time said bonnet was taken away, the said Collins and the countryman came in together, he the said Collins having with him the trunk of the said Ellen Griffin, which he the said Collins said he was going to deliver to the countryman for the purpose of indemnifying him for the money which had been stolen from him. That said Collins searched the said Ellen Griffin in his store, and took from her about eleven dollars which was alleged to have been part of the money stolen from the countryman, and as said Collins informed this deponent was delivered to said countryman.

That as Collins informed this deponent, he received from said countryman two dollars for his trouble in said business.

This deponent was prosecuted for said trunk and bonnet, but at the time they were not in his possession, nor did he know who had them. That Mr. Collins served the summons upon this deponent and at the time told this deponent, that he need not care nothing about it; and afterwards in a few days informed this deponent that the suit was settled, and further this deponent saith not.

John Cornell.

Sworn this 18*th day of July,* 1822, *before me. Henry Mead, Alderman, &c.*

CITY OF NEW-YORK, SS.

James Woods, of the said city, mate of a vessel, being duly sworn, saith, that by a base conspiracy of persons, he was arrested and imprisoned in the city prison or bridewell, of this city, and being there for three courts, he was put upon his trial and acquitted and discharged. That deponent employed George W. Niven, and William M. Price as his counsel, to defend him. That Mr. Niven was justly the favourite counsel generally of the prisoners in the part of the prison deponent was confined, and was generally recommended as counsel to those who might be brought there. First because every confidence was put in his ability, and assiduity in the preparing and trying causes, and secondly, because he was more liberal and faithful in preparing and attending to the trial of prisoners, who were put in prison without friends or means to employ counsel, than any other lawyer who practiced in the Court of Sessions. It being known to the prisoners that Mr. Niven would give every prisoner who should be so unfortunate as to be imprisoned without friends or money, as fair and full a defence as though he was paid, and evidence upon evidence proved the sincerity of Mr. Niven in that particular. Thirdly, because Mr. Niven refused on all occasions to flatter prisoners, but told them openly their situation, and often advised them to keep the money offered as a fee, as he could do nothing for them, and they would by giving their money to counsel throw it away. And this deponent further saith, that for those reasons he did from time to time recommend Mr. Niven as counsel, as well to those as were able to pay, as those who who were unable to pay, and they were all treated with the same attention, and frequently Mr. Niven has over and above his professional services expended money out of his own pocket gratuitously in aid of poor prisoners defence. That for the whole period of time this deponent was a prisoner, he never knew any prisoner complain or exhibit any dissatisfaction at the conduct of Mr. Niven, though from time to time for several weeks before deponents discharge, there was a jealousy in relation to Mr. Nivens practice as counsel, and every attempt was made by the principal keeper of the prison and his turnkey to destroy the practice of Mr. Niven in the prison. On one occasion this deponent recommended Mr. Niven to one of his fellow prisoners as counsel, which came to the knowledge of the principal keeper, his interrogating the man until he told him. When the keeper called deponent and told him. that if he recommended Mr. Niven as counsel to any of the prisoners, he would put deponent in close confinement, which deponent understood to be in the dungeon; and afterwards said keeper came in the inside of the prison and told the prisoners that Mr. Niven was no better than any other lawyer, with a view to dissuade the prisoners from employing Mr. Niven, and afterwards threatened all the prisoners that if any one mentioned the name of Mr. Niven, or recommend him in any way as counsel, he would put such person in the dungeon. And this deponent further saith, that when this hostility of the keeper and his turnkeys first commenced in relation to Mr. Niven, the turnkeys also commenced offering to get the prisoners out and receive pay for it, and utterly in all cases refused to send any letters or word to the friends of the prisoners, or to aid them in any way, unless they were paid in advance, and in one case this deponent was informed, and believes by one of his fellow prisoners, that he had paid one of the turnkeys fifteen dollars, to obtain his discharge, and he was discharged. And this deponent further saith, that prisoners have frequently applied to the turnkeys for the benefit of counsel, when they were told they did not want counsel, and their application refused. And this deponent further saith, that he knew one of the turnkeys to receive in one morning, five dollars from five prisoners, to get discharged, and one of them had no money when the turnkey told him he would lock him up if he did not pay the dollar, and one of the five told the turnkey he would pay it for him when he went down stairs, and the man was let out, and further this deponent saith not.

James Wood.

Sworn before me this 24tth day of January, 1822. *Wm. Lowerie, commissioner under act of March* 24, 1818

CITY AND COUNTY OF NEW-YORK, SS.

Eben J. S. Bell of the City of New-York, being duly sworn, saith, that he, deponent, was a prisoner confined in the city prison for about seven or eight weeks, on charges of purchasing stolen goods, &c. That he, deponent, employed George W. Niven and William M. Price as his counsel. And this deponent further saith, that by conspiracies of individuals, there were several indictments found by the Grand Jury against him, deponent, which enlarged the bail so much as to prevent his procuring bail. That several of the said indictments were tried and this deponent was honourably acquitted, when the district attorney, under the advice of the court, abandoned the others, and this deponent was discharged. That while the deponent was a prisoner as aforesaid, Mr. Niven was frequently sent for: prompt attention to his clients, and more particularly his promptness and attention to the cases of prisoners who had no friends nor means to pay counsellors, from whom he could not expect ever to be remunerated, endeared the prisoners to him, and he was therefore the favorite counsellor in the hall of the prison where deponent was confined; and this deponent further saith, that on an average, there is only one out of ten prisoners in the city prison, that are able to pay any fee whatever to counsel, and that all those who applied to Mr. Niven shared the same attention in their business, whether rich or poor, and deponent and his fellow prisoners, were informed and believed by prisoners charged with crime, and so poor, as not to be able to pay even the expences for subpœnas for their witnesses; that Mr. Niven when he thought them innocent and oppressed, has advanced the money out of his own pocket and procured the attendance of their witnesses, tried their causes as counsel, and often had such persons acquitted. And this deponent has been informed by his fellow prisoners, and believes, that Mr. Niven has furnished to indigent prisoners, clothing to make them comfortable under their confinement; that this deponent had an opportunity to be acquainted with the acts of Mr. Niven as counsel in the prison, and the opinions of the prisoners generally; and that no act of Mr. Niven's was at any time ever considered censurable, but he was justly considered the friend and benefactor of those who were so unfortunate as to be confined there, in procuring them a fair and full trial. And this deponent further saith, that the liberal course of conduct pursued by Mr. Niven, had its tendency to break up a system of extortions and speculations carried on in said prison, with those whom misfortune had placed there. And this deponent further saith, that he has known prisoners confined under what is termed "examination" to be refused the benefits of counsel, and in many instances where in such cases application has been made to the keeper of the prison and turnkeys, that the applicant has been threatened with confinement in the *chain room* and the *dungeon*, if the request should be repeated, which has frequently deterred persons so confined from repeating their requests. Deponent has frequently heard the keeper and his turnkeys to persons so confined, ridicule the idea of employing counsel, alleging that they could send for any thing the prisoners wanted, and they might as well pay one as another and deponent at same time, understood and believes that persons sent to the prison as paupers and as disorderly persons were so employed by the keepers in such speulations out of prisoners And this deponent further saith, that James Gilchrist and Thomas Densmore the turnkeys of said prison, are constantly in the habit of dissuading prisoners from employing counsel and flattering them, that they can get them released, if the prisoners would pay them, which was frequently done by both of them, and this deponent further saith, the conduct of the keeper and his turnkeys was usually so violent, abusive and tyrannical as to prevent the friends and relations of the prisoners so unfortunately confined, from bringing them victuals and necessaries, at the hours set for that purpose, and to such an extent as to deter them from coming at all to minister to their comfort or relief. And this deponent further saith, that the principal keeper made a rule, that he would put in the chain room or in the dungeon, any one of the prisoners, who at any time, would dare to advise or recommend any lawyer to his fellow prisoners, and finding that the liberal conduct of Mr. Niven would put down the speculations of his turnkeys out of the prisoners. His threats were made more particularly to the prisoners against mention being made of the name of Mr. Niven, and would often urge to them that Mr. Niven was no better than other lawyers, who if they sent for could see them. And this deponent further saith, that the keeper made a rule that instead of counsel having the privilege of coming to the bar of the prison, giving to each prisoner, the right to emyloy counsel or not, Every prisoner when counsel should wish to see them, would be called out of prison ; the operation of which rule, was, that those who had no means to retain counsel would shrink from sending for any, and instead of having the benefit of the liberality of counsel, as before then introduced by Mr. Niven ; they were frequently called out into court without their witnesses or any previous advice or preparation of their cases, and convicted, which rule of the keeper, was generally understood in the prison as meant to

shut out counsel from having free access to prisoners, the more effectually to enable the turnkeys to do the double duty of counsel and keepers, and to make money by obtaining through the police the discharges of those put in for small offences and this deponent further saith not. E. I. S. Bell.
Sworn before me, this 18th day of Feb. 1822. Wm. Lowerie, *Commissioner under act of March 24, 1818.*

CITY OF NEW-YORK, SS.

William Wiley of said city, being duly sworn, doth depose and say, that he has had conversations with John Davenport, a butcher in Washington-market since the twenty ninth day of May last, in relation to a certain affidavit made by the said John Davenport in relation to George W. Niven Esq. that he the said Davenport informed this deponent that the affidavit so made by him was not voluntary on his part, but that he had been called upon, and sent for by Josiah Hedden, Esq. before he could be prevailed upon to make the same. That he intended to make no complaint against Mr. Niven, but that John S. Dusenbury frequently entreated him, and told him he would be be compelled to make it, and accordingly presented to him the annexed subpoena under the hand and seal of Josiah Hedden, Esq. one of the police magistrates. That pursuant to the said subpoena, he did go to the police officer, when his affidavit was taken by Mr. Stevens in the presence of said Hedden, and which would not have been done unless he had been served with compulsory process, for that purpose, and further the deponent saith not. W. Wiley.
Sworn this 16th day of July 1822, before me, Cornelius Roosa, Com.

The Subpœna was in the common printed form, as follows;
CITY AND COUNTY OF NEW-YORK, SS.
The people of the state of New-York,
To John Davenport,
We command and firmly enjoin you and each of you, that laying all other matters aside, and notwithstanding any excuse you and each of you be in your proper persons before the special justices at the police office in the city hall of New-York, on the 29th day of May, 1822, at 11 o'clock, in the forenoon of that day, to testify and give evidence in a complaint for a misdemeanour, made by the people against George W. Nevin.
Given under my hand and seal, the 29th day of May one thousand eight hundred and twenty-two. J. Hedden.

We do certify, that we have been for a number of years acquainted with George W. Niven, Esqr. and have never discovered any dishonourable proceedings on his part in his professional practice with us, but on the contrary have found him therein liberal and correct.
May 31st, 1822.
John Anthon, David Graham, E. W. King, J. Warren Brackett, Robert Bogardus, David Brush, F. A. Tallmadge, John

Towt, A. Hegeman, J. L. Riker, Roswell W. Lewis, E. Slosson, W. F. Osgood, James M'Kueen, John M. Macdonald, Charles G. Ferris, H. Scove l, J. Hammond, John Leveridge, George Wilson, William Lowerie, Alexander L. M'Donald, Richard J. Wells, Jacob Wyckoff, E. T. Pinckney, Wm. Wiley, Charles G. Haines, John L. Graham, Charles Graham, William M. Price, D. Codwise, A. Sherman, J. Tucker, Robert L Wilson, P. G. Hildreth, W. T. M Coun, D. Randell, Samuel Osgood, W. A. Thompson, R. Swanton, Joseph D. Fay, S Cowdrey, Wm. W. M'Clelan, W. L. Morris, H. M. Western, James L. Bell.

Belmont, July 10th, 1822,

GEORGE W. NIVEN, ESQR.

Dear sir, your letter of July 2d, would have been answered by me before this time, but I have not had an opportunity until this day to convey a letter to you, this may appear strange to you, but my time and the time of my people, is so much occupied, that we visit New-York city as seldom as some persons who live much more remote.

I am extremely sorry to find by your letter, that you are engaged in a controversy with persons who you say act with malignity towards you, it is better at all times to be at peace if possible, but if a man is attcked no matter from what quarter, it is his bounden duty to make a most manly resistance, be the event what it may. So much for general principles, and now for your case.

The nature of the controversy with whom it exists or how it has been brought about, is a thing altogether unknown to me; about that therefore, I shall not say any thing. As it regards your professional labours since you have practiced at the New-York bar, I think I can say with safety, that in all cases where your practice came under my view, you appeared to conduct with an honourable liberality, and at the same time a due regard to the interest of your client, which certainly placed you high in my good opinion.

Yours with much regard, James L. Bell.

CITY OF NEW-YORK, SS.

Harmanus Tallman, of said city, coroner, being duly sworn saith, that he is acquainted with John Davenport, of the said city, butcher, in the Washington Market. that he has known him for eight years last past, and that he is a man of good moral character, and full faith and credit is due to him as a man of veracity. Harmanus Tallman.

Sworn this 13th day of June, 1822, Stephen Allen.

CITY OF NEW-YORK, SS.

George Hodgson, of the said city, grocer, being duly sworn, saith, that he is well acquainted with the above named John

Davenport, and has been so acquainted with him for three years las past, and that he is a man of good moral character, and is entitled to full faith and credit under his oath.

George Hodgson.

Sworn this 17th day of June, 1822. *Stephen Allen.*

CITY OF NEW-YORK, SS.

Smith Cutter, of the said city, physician, being sworn, saith, that he has known John Davenport, of the said city, butcher for several years past and belives him entitled to full faith and credit under his oath.

Smith Cutter.

Sworn this 22d day of June, 1822. *Stephen Allen.*

Mr. *Maxwell* then offered an affidavit of Doctor Kissam, touching the affairs of Latimer, which Mr. Nivens counsel objected to, the court having ruled, that no new affidavit touching this matter should be introduced against him, because the records of acquittal were conclusive evidence that he was not guilty of the charges to which this affidavit related.

Mr. *Wilkins* said, this affidavit was only offered as confirmation of that of Mr Latimer, and insisted upon the authority of the case of the *King against Sutherland.*

First Judge We have considered this point, and think that this case differs from the case cited as to the conclusiveness of the acquittal. If the judge of the supreme court had thought proper to set the enquiry on foot, or the supreme court had instituted any enquiry, it would have been like that case, but no such thing was done, and we do not think it proper for us to open it.

Mr. *Maxwell* then stated the authorities of law on which he meant to rely.

Loft 271, to show that an attorney is under the control of the court, in respect to matters not directly in the line of his business as an attorney, because he gains credit with the public by the licence of the court.

2 *Wilson* 382, That where an attorney does any thing wrong any where as attorney, the superior court will interfere.

Dougl. 357, An application to be admitted, a barrister refused, because the party applying was insolvent, and had become security for morethan he was worth.

2 *Atk* 173, where a Mr. justice Mitchel, a barrister of the degree of sergeant, was silenced for mal-practice in contriving the marriage of a ward of the court of chancery, and where it is said, that had he been a solicitor, the ready and proper way would have been to have struck him off the roll.

1 *Stra.* 384, Where two persons had put in bail in feigned names, and because they could not be prosecuted on the stat. 21, James 1. c 26, the court ordered them and the attornies to be set in the pillory, which was accordingly done.

1 *Wils* 22. An attorney fined and imprisoned for taking £200 of one charged with forgery for letting him out of the hands of a tipstaff.

2 *Roll R.* 459. That the court would strike an attorney off the roll for altering a paper book without leave.

Cro. ch. 74. An attorney put out of the roll, and cast over the bar, and committed to the fleet, for suing a *capias* in debt without an original, because against his oath, that he should not practice any deceit. And one of the Common Pleas put out of the roll and thrown over the bar, and fined £5 and sworn never to practice as an attorney, and to be brought to the king's bench bar, and the exchequer, that knowledge was to be taken of him, that he was not to practice any more in those courts, which was for falsifying a *capias*.

1 *Cowp.* 824. An attorney convicted of a felony, was struck off the roll, though he had been burned in the hand, and suffered imprisonment pursuant to his sentence *five years* before, and no misconduct imputed to him since, not by way of punishment but as being an unfit person to practice as an attorney. The complaint was by the magistrates of the county to prevent the neighbourhood from receiving an injury. Lord Mansfield considering it for the dignity of the profession, consulted all the judges, and solemnly delivered their unanimous opinion.

6 *Mod.* 187, *per Holt.* If an attorney will take a man's money to do business, and does not do it, we may enter into a summary examination of it, and if we find him refractory we may strike him off the roll.

6 *East* 142. One Southerton an attorney, was prosecuted and acquitted of threatening to set on foot a prosecution for penalties. And though the offence could not be brought within the statute or common law, and the attorney was acquitted of the indictment, Yet, as enough appeared to satisfy the court that he was an improper person to remain as an attorney on the rolls of the court, a rule was made to show cause to which he yielded, and was accordingly struck off the roll, his counsel admitting that he could not resist it.

1 *L. N. Y. Act concerning counsellors, attornies, and solicitors*, *v* 5, *p.* 417. "That if any counsellor, attorney or solicitor be found notoriously in default of record, or otherwise guilty of any deceit, mal-practice, or misdemeanour, he may be suspended or put out of the roll at the discretion of the court, &c.

The cause being now ready to be summed up, the court intimated that they would hear two counsel on each side, and afterwards hear Mr. Niven himself,

Mr. Anthon begged that all Mr. Niven's counsel might be heard; they were three, but by taking each a portion of the defence, as in the case of impeachments is usual, the arguments would not be prolonged. And Mr. Price said the like indulgence had once been granted to Mr. Jacob Barker.

The Recorder expressed his opinion that all should be heard.

Mr. Anthon contended for the right of opening and closing, as in cases of showing cause against a new trial or attachment.

First Judge. This inquiry was instituted by the court, and the court assigned counsel to carry on the inquiry, Mr. Niven was called on to show cause by the rule of this court, he has read affidavits. Others have been read against him, and, upon the whole, we think, that his counsel should open, and he be allowed to close.

Mr. Anthon wished, that as the party himself was very much exhausted, one of his counsel should be heard in reply in his stead.

First Judge. If he is so exhausted we will give him time.

General Bogardus said he had advised his client to go home, because he did not think he could have staid five minutes longer on account of the state of his health, and the exhaustion under which he laboured.

Mr. Wilkins. Perhaps these repeated delays may lead us to the new constitution, and the change of system.

General Bogardus answered that this was a case too serious for wit or pleasantry. If Mr. Niven was to reply, he certainly ought to hear all that was said against him.

The court then determined, that no other affidavits should be read on either side, and adjourned till Wednesday the 24th inst. at 11 o'clock A. M.

July 24, 1822.

On this day the counsel proceeded to sum up, and observe upon the evidence before the court.

Mr. Anthon, on behalf of Mr. Niven, began by drawing a distinction between the case of a counsel, and that of an attorney, and contended, that they were by no means subject to the same discipline. He imputed the prosecution of those charges against his client to the officious and extraordinary zeal of the police magistrates, and the extraordinary interference of the grand jury to the impressions received from a quarter too likely to prevail with them; and to prejudices imbibed from other sources than the evidence before them. Those who sought to mortify and injure Mr. Niven, had reason to triumph. Mr. A. then proceeded to examine the eight distinct heads of accusation which now appeared by so many affidavits to constitute the whole body of his offences; and first, as to Stivers. Certainly any comparison or conflict between this gentleman and Stivers, was sufficiently degrading to satisfy the malice of any enemy, without going a step further. This man's affidavit, and all the others upon which the charges were founded were drawn up in the police office, so that the whole was resolvable into a mere contention between him and the police. With respect to Stivers judging by his first, second, and third affidavit, he must be either a being destitute of understanding, or of any moral sense. He was charged with stealing, he employed Mr. Niven as his counsel to defend him, and agreed to give him a fee of 25 dollars; but having no money, gave him an order for certain furniture that was not in use. Then he comes on pretence that no services had been rendered him, and that he was discharged without a trial, and tenders five dollars, and demands a return of the goods he had before given to his counsel. Now, it is settled law, that a counsel fee is an honourary gift, and can never be recovered back. This law is ancient and universal; we derive it from ancestors who derived it from the Roman annals. But, because he would not deliver back this gift, or this pledge. whichever it was, a complaint is made against him in a criminal court, and that court being incompetent to notice it, it is made to travel into this court, which is of a civil jurisdiction, and has taken a new form. It has been decided, that where a counsel has received his fees, but is unable to attend to the businesss, no action will lie to recover these fees back from him, because it is a vested gift. Whether he will return his fee, or any part of it, depends entirely on his own disposition and discretion. But whether he does, or does not choose to do so, the court cannot, for that, strike his name out of their roll. But here Mr. Niven swears positively, that he did render services to this Stivers, that he attended at the trial, and had his name struck out of the indictment; and as to his taking his goods instead of money, as a fee, he did it reluctantly, and not till the prisoner told him, that the police had taken all his money from him: and he continued to refuse till the wretched man requested him, with tears in his eyes, to accept of his offer. It may, perhaps, be said, that if he was moved by compassion, he might have shown it better by acting gratuitously. Counsel may volunteer, so may men of every other calling give away their time, their labour, or their capital: But, if the daily labour of the counsel, is the daily bread of his family, there is no court that can compel him to give that away. But I have said more than enough, considering that in point of fact this witness appears, in every aspect, unworthy of credit or attention, when he comes as an accuser of any body whatsoever, for he not only stands confessed a thief, and an approver, but one that has made three affidavits successively contradicting the one the other.

2dly. The next accuser is Mr. Kerland. This counterfeiter was in gaol, and very anxious to procure bail, and he gave Mr. Niven, as a fee, an order for five dollars, which his friend would not honour. Having no credit, he offers a pledge and gives a trunk of clothing worth   dollars, considering that he had engaged Mr. Niven to act not only for himself, but for his friend and accomplice Stuart, he has little reason to complain of being overreached. But, allowing that Mr. Niven had not exerted himself as he did for either of these compeers, still the effects were given and received as a counsel fee, and admitting that he effected nothing for Stuart, and that Kerland had been discharged without his interference, still it was his due.

3dly. Charley, the counterfeiter, accuses Mr. Niven of having withheld his watch after he had received the five dollars. He thinks the watch should be returned, because he did not earn it. Mr Niven thinks otherwise, but this is no place to settle that difference. An action of trover and conversion, is the proper way to try such questions ; but here can be no question, for Mr. Niven shows, that this man was tried, that he defended him. and that he was acquitted.

So far went the evidence on which the presentment of the grand jury was founded, and were the inquiry should have stopped, since the grand jury presented nothing else.

It is to be observed also, that all the complaints here are made by clients, and all are revelations of what passed between these clients and their counsel. Here then is a dangerous kind of evidence where there is no reciprocity, no safety for the accused. The silence and secrecy imposed upon the counsel is the privilege of the client not of the counsel. The client may disclose what he chuses, and conceal what he chuses, whereas the counsel cannot even when attacked in his reputation, by an ungrateful, malicious or suborned client betray his secrets. If the mouth of such a client is opened whilst that of the counsel is closed, the counsel is left entirely at his mercy. Therefore, neither should be allowed to make disclosures, and this affidavit should be suppressed or entirely disregarded. 4thly. Covenhoven's affidavit wants the main thing, without which no testimony can ever obtain credit, it wants good faith. He remembers all that is necessary for the accusation of Mr. Niven, but says nothing of the facts that go to discharge him. Mr. Niven, however, shows that he was an ancient client, and that he owed him $45, at the same time that he complains of him for not paying him $40.

5thly. Shoemaker comes next in order. Who is he? A mayor, a merchant, a lawyer, a broker, a Caleb Quotem. His character has been impeached, and though there has been abundance of time to support his credit, no attempt has been made: It was too desperate to venture. It is true his testimony amounts to little, even supposing him to be a credible person. One Peers was charged with stealing, bail was to be procured, the prisoner was to run away, and the court of exchequer was to be solicited for remission of the forfeiture. In England, we find that counsel give ingenious advice how to trick the court and save the client, and much more artifice than this is allowed to pass without censure, nay even with applause. This however, was the suggestion of the client himself, Mr. Niven only followed up his suggestions. He was asked, what would be the consequence to the bail, if the principal should run away, and he answered very truly that he would have to pay the amount in the recognizance, unless he could prevail with the exchequer to remit it. But if this really was a crime sufficient to justify throwing of a counsellor over the bar upon the authority of English precedents, it should be remembered that in England the client would not be allowed to betray his counsel's secrets, no more than the counsel would be allowed to disclose his.

6thly. As to Ellen Griffin, this inhabitant of Bancker-street was sentenced to six months confinement in the penitentiary. Such a witness required some support undoubtedly, but like all the rest she remains entirely unsupported, and uncorroborated. This convicted prostitute employed Mr. Niven to endeavour at obtaining her pardon, and having no money, she gave him articles of clothing worth ten dollars. He was unsuccessful, for she had no merit to entitle her to any favour, and the releasing such as she turned out to be, would be like opening the prison doors to all offenders At the expiration of her term she comes out. Collins is then sent to demand the property, and when he finds Mr. Niven disposed to deliver it up, declines taking it, saying he will call again; but he never did call again, which shows that it was a refusal he wanted, and not a redelivery of the goods. This is fully charged upon him in Mr. Niven's affidavit, and he has not made any answer to this charge.

7thly. In Latimer's case, the indictment which he prosecuted against Mr. Niven was removed by *certiorari* and tried before Mr. Justice Yates. Latimer was cross-examined, and made himself so ridiculous that the jury acquitted Mr. Niven. This unkennelled fox is then taken to a private chamber, where there was no cross examination to detect him, and a consistent story being written down, he swears that it is all true. If, after a full acquittal, these attacks were to be at any distance of time renewed in such a shape as this, and the verdict of acquittal was not to be held conclusive, there would be no safety for any man. An inveterate prosecutor would only have to watch till the lapse of time would have swept away all the defendants evidence, or till he could form some new combination, and the man whom his country had pronounced not guilty upon the open testimony of his accuser, would fall before the pen of the ready writer.

As to the case cited from 6 East, it is an authority for, and not against us, inasmuch as the judge who tried the indictment did not think proper to pass any censure nor make any representation touching any misconduct of the defendant, and in this the cases are clearly distinguishable. If the judge of the Supreme Court who had before him the prosecutor, the case, and the defendant, did not interfere, certainly no Inferior Court should interpose in that behalf, and this court will not.

8thly. The last head of accusation is the affidavit of Mr. Davenport the butcher. By the *jurat* it appears to have been taken at the police, and there is so much the more reason that the party should be protected by this court. If all the parties had been citizens who came voluntarily forward I should not have made this observation, but knowing the nature of the contest, and the circumstances of the case I am compelled to it as an act of duty. This man was subpœnaed to appear and give evidence in a matter to be tried between the people and George W. Niven: there was no such matter, and the court seeing the cloven foot are bound to be on their guard, and to use their good judgment in discriminating between the story of an expert penman whose feelings flow with his ink, and the tongue of a self convicted accuser when put to the test of a cross-examination. The charge set forth is, that he employed Mr. Niven to bring a suit for a small sum, and that he made him pay twice the amount for his fees, but why does he not tell the whole truth, that he pocket the whole of that money Mr. Niven's fees and all. He suppresses the essential part of the story, and thereby loses all credit, since the maxim is, that suppression of the truth amounts to the allegation of a falsehood.

Thus every one of the witnesses stands obnoxious to discredit on their own oaths: let the counsel by their eloquence white wash them as they may. So far from Mr. Nivens having received $25 fee, and $25 costs, Mr. Davenport knew that when he sued Mr. Niven for his beef, the set off of the counsel fee was objected to, and, that of that fee he has been literally cheated. Here then is a counsellor at law charged by eight witnesses all without character. The counsel knew these objections would be made, but they could not mend their case. One only of these witnesses (William Davenport,) is supported, but it is by two persons not appearing before this court, and of whose own character we know nothing. What we claim then for our client, is what the meanest culprit is entitled to that his prosecutors shall make out their case by creditable testimony.

The counsel seem to rely on the chapter read from Beccaria, but their logic is fallacious, "we have charged you with malpractices, therefore you are a criminal, and being a criminal you are not to be believed, upon your oath. This may be law in Italy, but our law is, that every man till he is convicted is presumed to be innocent: and that is the law that will govern this court, and its decisions.

The counsel have alluded to the case of the indictment against Mr. Niven. They are welcome to read that case if they will read also, that the jury pronounced the whole charge to be false and groundless.

The only charge substantiated, is that he took goods in pledge for his fees. This is what every counsel would not do: but the necessities of all are not equally urgent. And as to receiving specific gifts, not in money, but in goods and effects, it is nothing new, it is a practice which we can trace back to the annals of Imperial Rome, where men of consular and senatorial dignity, did not think themselves degraded by it. Cicero was enriched by such presents, jewels, garments, furniture, farms, villas; none were rejected. And low and degraded as these inmates of the bridewell may be, they too are entitled to have their counsel, and if they have no money, or if their money be taken from them, they may give, pledge, or mortgage their effects. Mortgages on real property have been taken by our most eminent counsel to secure their more ample compensation, and it cannot be a crime to take a smaller pledge for a smaller fee. Nor is it for any tribunal to interfere between the counsel and the client, and say whether the client has overrated or underrated the talents and exertions of his counsel.

This gentleman has pursued a profession, which cannot be attained or exercised but to the exclusion of all others, and is at a time of life when he can not readily change his habits or pursuits.

If he is deprived or degraded but for one day, it may result in the beggary of himself and his family. Is such a sentence to be pronounced upon the testimony of notorious thieves, and common prostitutes. Shall he, who was admitted to the bar and stands approved on the certificates of eminent counsel, be degraded from it and disqualified by rogues and counterfeiters.

General Bogardus. I shall present to the court three points, which if decided in favour of Mr. Niven, would put an end to the question, and shut out a great deal of tedious and unprofitable inquiry.

1st. That a counsellor is not liable for any advice he may have given, nor any fee he may have received, nor for any mode of securing it, is proved by the silence of the statute and the absence of any decision. Counsel in the upper parts of this state, are in the daily practice of receiving commodities instead of money for their fees; and one of the judges of the Supreme Court observed to me, that if taking such compensation was to be a cause of disbarring a lawyer, that every one of those gentlemen would be turned over the bar.

2dly. No one of all the acts charged by the prosecutors of this complaint, was done in capacity of attorney, of the Court of Common Pleas, in the city of New-York.

If this be not an answer, it must follow, that every act of every attorney is inquirable in this form, and the attorney instead of having the benefit of the trial by jury, is put out of the protection of the constitution and the law. Nor is it altogether by reason of his licence in this court, that he practices in the sessions, for he may practice there, without being attorney or counsel of any court as a mere by-stander may, if the court should choose to hear what he had to say.

3dly. All the affidavits disclose conversations and secrets of clients, and if these were admitted, the independence of the profession would be at an end, for the counsel is bound to keep the secrets of his clients, and if he cannot reply without disclosing them, he is exposed, by that privilege of the client to be the victim of that privilege : and your honors, who are of the profession, could never hold the stations you have done at the bar, if you had not on some occasions conversed with your clients in a way that you would not wish your clients to reveal, nor any body else to hear or know. But as there are many on the bench. who do not understand questions of law, nor the rules of the profession, I shall not altogether rely upon these points, but do my duty, which is a voluntary one, and proceed to examine the facts.

I do not dispute that courts may censure or punish attornies, nor even counsel where there are flagrant acts of professional misconduct. But as there is a written statute upon that subject, the road is traced for them, and our statute does not apply in this case, because, at the same time, that we admit the authority of the court, we insist, that under the statute, the party, before the court can proceed to exercise that authority, must have had a trial, and been found guilty: and we are not to be guided by what has been done in foreign courts, nor take the law from the mouths of judges who sit to administer justice under a different system. The district attorney, when he read from Beccaria, should have seen, that it made against himself, for that Mr. Niven was not a criminal whose oath was not to be believed, but that his witness, Stivers, and that prostitute, were convicts by record and confession: and though Charley escaped, yet there is pretty strong evidence that he was of that class contemplated by the author. Davenport, also, has gone pretty near the edge, for he sold the drover's beef, pocketed the price, and paid the drovers with the insolvent act. In Tidd's Practice, vol. 1. page 257, it is said, that where the attorney denies the fraud or mal-practice, on his oath, he shall be discharged: but I admit, there may be crimes so disgraceful, as to warrant the striking an attorney off the roll, though the acts were not done in the same court. For instance, some have said, that a riot in a church might warrant such a measure, others have said, that if men be not honourable, as well as honest, they may be striken off, and that some judge had so expressed himself. But I think judges go far enough in holding men to be honest, without making them what is called honourable; for that word would require a legislative definition. Some think, that killing men is honourable, and that not to kill them is dishonourable. Some think, that it is dishonourable not to pay a gambling, or a whoreing debt, but that to cheat a taylor or a shoemaker, is nothing dishonourable. The counsel here referred to the case of Walter Wood who was censured for purchasing at a sheriff's sale, but was not for that struck off the roll; and to the case of Elisha Williams, and that of Mr. Mitchell of Westchester, where it never occurred to the court to strike the attorney off the roll. And let the court reflect, that no jury has found Mr. Niven guilty of a crime, that the sentence they are called upon to pass is next to death, and the court will stop, no doubt, to inquire first, whether they have such jurisdiction. If I have any fears, that the court would do so, and I own I am not without them, it is not that I feel any conviction of my client's guilt; but my fears arise from the prejudices which prevail against him, and the power which operates against him. I have known of two indictments against gentlemen of this bar; but there was no such zeal for conviction, one of them was disposed of without my knowledge, or that of three-fourths of the bar. How different the proceedings here. This presentment was not hushed or softened, it was twice read aloud in the hearing of the public, two gentlemen were assigned to carry it into effect, and I cannot help remarking, that no sooner were they assigned to institute the inquiry, than they came forward with budgets of papers ready prepared, and saying they had more affidavits to lay before the court.

Some judges of this court are said to have pronounced in the beginning, opinions very unfavourable to my client, in which, if so, they erred. The number of affidavits tumbling in from some manufactory, and the interference of the police, made me, and still cause me to fear. Though, I hope, that the court will not convict my client in an arbitrary mode, nor until they are fully convinced, that they have the power. And I will, I now have confidence. The charges against him are composed of such different materials and disconnected matters, as can hardly be reduced to any distinct points The court should, therefore, take them up as seperate charges, and decide upon them, severally, and not embody the whole: if taking them one by one, there is no one sufficient, then they are one by one to be laid aside, and the whole is a nullity. I shall then, summarily, examine the several pieces of testimony.

1st. The presentment is a self-created thing, the first of its kind, for no charge, in a court of justice, ought to be made for mere curiosity, without some legal form, or definite object. Nor have grand juries unlimited power They have no right to wound slander and libel, and judges ought to suppress such assumed authority, as was done in the case of Judge Tallmadge. They have no such power or authority. There is neither law or precedent for it. They may present things as nuisances, but they have no right to present persons. The court, however, have said, that the presentment was a suggestion to them, that it led them to the affidavits, and that they would look into them.

(The counsel then read the presentment, and observed) if a lawyer can be thus presented, where is the line drawn, why may not mayors, recorders, judges, aldermen, and other magistrates, be also presented? Why may they not also be abused and stigmatized by any two or three prostitutes or thieves? It is an awful consideration, and you are all exposed to it. If a thief, or prostitute, and a felon, twice brought before justice. for counterfeit money, can thus jeopardise your safety and your reputation, better never have been members of any court of justice, for having reached fifty years of age you may receive a taint by which your former life will be tarnished, and the residue a drug. This grand jury say, that Mr. Niven has been addicted to similar misdemeanors, and that they had this information from authentic sources. It is a subject of great regret, that these " truths do not come within the pale of an indictment." No doubt they do regret it, and they have done all they could to lessen their regret, but three of them certify, in terms unequivocal, that no affidavit, or no proof, from any source, was laid before them, other than the three affidavits. Why then do they talk of their official information from official sources? These three show, that that part of the presentment is not founded in truth. So much for that honourable body of men stiled *grand*, who are not for being brought there together one bit greater or grander than when they were pursers on board of a ship, or working in their counting houses.

Stivers, the veriest tool that ever was moulded in the forge of a police, was one of these witnesses. If they catch him every day, they will have every day an affidavit, for or against, according to the party that gets hold of him. Mark the words that have been put into his mouth. They make him speak of the bank robber, a word much likelier to be that of some other invention than his. At the foot of what is written he sets his mark, and whoever penned the affidavit, he is ready to swear to it. Mr. Niven, surprised, goes to him to ask the reason; he says he never intended to swear to such facts, and a statement being drawn up. he goes to the judge and swears, that the former was all a falsehood, and that he never intended to make such an affidavit. The police again catch him, and he swears. At the same time that the first affidavit was on its travels, or in the hands of the Supreme Court, they make him swear, that all the facts in his second affidavit are untrue. Now, you cannot believe them all; you cannot choose among them, for you cannot tell which to believe, and there is no safety but in discrediting them all.

As to Kerland's affidavit, it would not, if true, support this proceeding, but every fact in it is disproved by Mr. Niven's oath, the one swearing, that the facts did, and the other, that they did not take place.

William Charley cannot be believed; he is charged with stealing, or receiving, three razors, worth three shillings, and he lies in jail for want of bail; and no one person can be got to give him countenance or character of any kind. He swears, that a watch cost him four pounds ten shillings, in England, which Mr. Field swears was not worth more than ten dollars. And, very strange to tell, after Mr. Niven had told him that all hell cannot save him, he sells his gun to raise a fee for the man that tells him so. If, indeed, the police are reduced to the necessity of working the destruction of George W. Niven, they have a mighty host at their command. They are governors and commanders of those who have no conscience, nor no faith, nor any fear before their eyes, but that of the police. Possessing the power of sending them to bridewell, they may wield them as they think fit.

If Edward Couhenhoven be the person I once knew, how he could be made such a tool, is, indeed, strange. (Mr. Niven observed, that that was his father.) I thought it could not be the same that I had known at Sing-Sing. See what a story his is. Five years ago they had business. Mr. Niven had three suits for him, and one in the Supreme Court. And after five years, he comes with this story of Mr. Niven's having no claim or demand upon him, which Mr. Niven denies, and which stands, besides, contradicted by records of courts, and is every particle disproved, as well by documentary, as personal proof, except, perhaps, this much, that his name is Couhenhoven.

If Mr. Shoemaker be the person he is represented and sworn

to be, before this court, the police deserve reproof. Here is a vagabond that has gone through every grade and condition, mayor, doctor, broker, lawyer, merchant, &c. &c who lies on the floor of a lawyer's office, by the indulgence of a boy that sweeps it, that he may not freeze in the street. And the very office where this beggar lays him down through the charity of the boy who sweeps that office, is the same. No. 19 Murray-Street, where this "merchant" is described in the affidavit, as having his residence, or domicil. Does not this police require correction? This merchant, however, is proved, by the oaths of Mr. Osgood, and Mr. Holden, to be utterly unworthy of credit.

The next is Ellen Griffin. After the rogues, come their associates, the prostitutes. This one is stated, by the police, in writing, to be a common prostitute, sent without trial to the penitentiary. Now, let the gentlemen consult Beccaria, and tell us, that the oaths of culprits are not to be trusted.

Mr. Collins, as is common with those officers in such cases, became the trustee of the convicted prostitute, and he applies to Mr. Niven to try and get her out, and she transfers her property to him. This was a mortal affront to attempt to change this venerable custom, and this officer resists till suit is brought. (This appearing to be a mistake, the counsel being apprised of it, continued.) No, he was not sued, it was not he, but Cornell that was sued, but, considering the interest and connexion, it makes it nearly the same thing. The trunk is given up, finally, to Mr. Niven. Some part of the contents are given away, the rest are offered to be restored, but the offer not accepted. Was not the law open to the parties who complain? The Justices' Courts are open to all parties Though the facts were all true, this court has no call, nor no motive for interfering; but the facts are disproved by the oaths of two witnesses, and cannot be taken to be true.

As to the Latimer affair, so much was said about it, proceeding from this marble house, that if the house of Mr. Niven had been torn down, I should not have been surprised at it. It found its way to the grand jury, and a bill of indictment was found, but there Mr. Niven had a fair trial, and was acquitted upon the evidence of his accuser alone. But now they get that same accuser again in a secret place, and put down upon paper a consistent story, and make advantage of it here, not as evidence, for it is not to be received as such, but to get it read again, and published in this court. But this court has very properly ruled that, Mr. Niven having been tried and acquitted before a Judge of the Supreme Court, and that judge having seen or said nothing of any misconduct of the attorney, he is to go clear in this court of every such imputation. And besides this is now an affair of two years standing. Time in all criminal charges is important and courts will some cases imply even from a short lapse of time, that the charge is fabricated and trumped up for the new occasion, and this though no legislative act enforces that conclusion. Now here was an ancient controversy about accounts, and accountability, it was as yet unsafe to make this attack, he was not till now sufficiently bowed down by oppression; but we say that a charge of this nature having slept two years, is not now to be resuscitated, the more so as seven years of his life have been reviewed before this court, and though the power of the police has born hard against him, we have been able to show the whole of their stories to be fabrications.

Mr. Davenport swears, Mr. Niven cheated him, I say that it was he, that cheated Mr. Niven out of his fee of twenty-five dollars, which two witnesses have sworn that he justly earned and deserved, though the Marine Court could not allow it in the form of a set-off. But he contrived to catch him off the limits and have him sued! very well, and suppose that Mr. Niven believed him to be one of those that delude the country people, cheat tradesmen, and speculate upon other men's property, and abuse the indulgence of the law, of which there are too many, what should forbid an attorney to form a scheme to defeat such knavery, and make him pay his debts, and prevent his cheating honest men. If it be said, that this affects the security who may be innocent of the fraud, it may be asked in return why does that security take that responsibility, and are not these securities pretty well aware of the affairs of their principles, and pretty well indemnified, and do they not know that they are deliberately going security for rascals devoid of honesty, and binding themselves as instruments to enrich the spendthrift and the rogue, at the expense of the frugal and the honest man. Now is this such an indignity to this court as to call upon it to strike his name from off their roll. But the story is false, for both he and his brother who is now in the western part of Pennsylvania, swear that he was unconscious of the act, and that it was Mr. Henry K. Niven who upon seeing Davenport off the limits, ordered the suit to be brought, without any contrivance on the part of his brother.

The judgment which is invoked against my client is one, that will overwhelm him, and his family. It affects him more than death, for after it is pronounced he will live a burthen to himself, and an eyesore to his friends, and therefore I offer no apology for the zeal which I may have shown in his defence.

The police of this city, was some time ago as good as ever had been in any, and except in this one instance, I have not altered my opinion of it. They may have been attacked or assailed by Mr. Niven, and may think that they are acting in their own defence, but no men ought to use the power of their office to destroy even in self defence. I have heard that one judge had said, that either the police or Mr. Niven must give way. If this be so in fact, it is a proof that the police is rotten and corrupt, and that it must, and will be broken up. I confine my observations to the facts in this case, I know of nothing else, but here is documentary proof that cannot be mistaken, and the case stands thus. Mr. Niven is charged with misdemeanors and put to answer for them, he has no process to compel witnesses to testify the truth, he applies to the court, and your honour says to him we have no way to compel your witnesses, we cannot assist you. The affidavits against you are all voluntary. Yet we find at the same time that subpœnas are issued, compelling persons by the force of official power to come forward and accuse. Now if it is come to this, that they are driven to such measures for their own defence, it is time they should be removed. But I hope it is not so, and that justice can be done to my client without changing the police, and in that hope I rest.

Mr. Price. The novel and peculiar situation of my client creating the deepest interest in the result of this trial, if so it may be called, cannot but account for the solicitude of council in his behalf.

Mr. Niven stands accused before this court, and called upon to answer at the peril of grevious pains and penalties, not for an offence to this court, nor for one which any other than a privileged citizen, could be called upon to answer in any court whatever.

The offence imputed, is, that my client has not professionally so conducted himself as to escape the disapprobation of his secret and concealed accusers. Indeed there is a generality in his accusation and a mystery in its prosecution well calculated to produce alarm. His offence has not the legal safety of a definition appertaining to it. A judgment against him even in this court of inferior jurisdiction, though it amount to a confiscation of his very means of living is unsusceptible of revision or correction. The chartered previleges of the vilest culprit are denied to him ; for this form of proceeding deprives him not only of the trial by jury, but of that more guarded constitutional provision, which professes to put him face to face with his accusers, and give him the benefit of cross-examining the witnesses against him. Nay, such is the peculiar condition of this trial, that he is not permitted to avail himself of your statute of limitation in criminal cases. His professional life has been ransacked for facts and cases, auxiliary to its destruction, and young as he is, the transactions of many years, are now by the accusing industry of his prosecutors, thrown upon him for explanation. He is put to his trial upon the testimony contained in these depositions, fearlessly penned, and fearlessly attested to. This court has not the advantage which every court and jury ought to have, of determining rightly of human testimony.—These paper witnesses are not put to the test.—The look, the gesture, the expression, which if publicly displayed, might perchance lead to the detection of those who would bear false witness, is in this mode of swearing covered up and concealed, by those who have wrecked their consciences on these depositions.

Aware that your honours have decided this to be a fit and proper mode of trial, I can of course submit such considerations with the single view of inviting greater caution in your decision. My client is to be tried as an attorney and counsellor of this court, and liable, it would seem, to be condemned for doing that *quasi attorney* which would be impunishable in any other relation of life.

It would be well therefore, to enquire a little of this office of attorney.—We have heard much of its priveleges and its honors—let us examine it.

An attorney of the court, was indeed formerly, a too much privileged officer, he could not be arrested, and held to bail if he was indebted to another, the ordinary process of law could not reach him—he must be proceeded against by bill; not as it now is, affording actual relief or payment of the due, but relief from the privilege which protected him, and upon such proceeding, the judgment was never immediatly effectual, but simply a forejudger of his privilege, whereupon he was liable to be proceeded against, as in ordinary cases. He might have been arrested, but upon motion to his court, he would have been released, and a writ of protection would have saved him harmless thereafter. So too with the office of counsellor—this in former times, was a degree so honorable, that the counsellor could not sue for his fee or recover it at law, for it was even defined to be *quiddum honorarium*, and not wages or hire which it would have been below his condition to have received. It is quite otherwise at present—a counsellor can now enforce the payment of his fee by action under the common counts, for work and labour done and performed. The privileges of these officers, are now useless or exploded, let us therefore have done with the illusion.—It is not competent now to say that a counsellor may not make his bargain for his compensation, as other individuals by law may do.

But it has been objected to Mr. Niven, that he charged too much. I have heard among ourselves, of one or two thousand dollars being freely given for arguing causes, that in point of time, would not engage the deliberation of a week—would you debar counsel who would make that bargain?. Are you as a court of justice, to enter into a nice enquiry of the value of such services, or are you rather to submit it to the intelligence of this community to decide which of the profession is entitled to the pounds, which to the shillings, and which to the pence, as a compensation. After the careful investigation which my associate counsel have made of the testimony in this case, it would be needless to enlarge upon it. The depositions of Couhenhoven and Davenport are contradicted or balanced by the testimony of those, who on the score of numbers or credit, are at least equally entitled to your confidence. As it respects Stivers, Kerland, or the theives or prostitutes from your prisons, who have weakly or wickedly assailled my client, I would not consent to waste a word upon them—in their own depositions they confess themselves tainted beyond the possibility of belief—they are both by profession and conviction, infamous in the sight of this court—and applying to them the ordinary rules of evidence, by which the vilest in your courts must be tried, they are utterly unworthy of credit.

. I do indeed seek the deliverance of my client from this most foul accusation, but I ask nothing in mercy towards him—and when I put before you the awful consequences of a judgment gaingt him, his former conduct, his family connections, his future prospects in life, it is but to invoke a careful and unbiased decision of his case.

The scandal which the weak or the wicked may have cast upon the profession to which he belongs, can surely never be attached to him, without that pure and conclusive testimony, which you would require for the sacrifice of any other member of the community.—Let him not I implore you, become the victim of public or private prejudice. You are indeed judges, but you are men also; your own inclinations, or the vicissitudes to which the affairs of this world are liable, may reduce you to that profession from which you have been called.—Judge ye then as ye would be judged.

Mr. MAXWELL.—IF IT PLEASE THE COURT,

I shall discharge the duty assigned me by the court with the mildness and forbearance which aggravated misconduct may allow—while I endeavour to do it in all brevity consistent with detailed and multiplied proofs.

That I shall speak of the respondent as he is, of his conduct as it deserves, in a fearless manner, I need hardly assure this court.

His threats, on any occasion, and in any place, I disregard—why should they affect me here, where fear never appalled any but the guilty?

The profession has suffered much from the misconduct of unworthy members emboldened by impunity, deriving greater confidence from the indifference of the bar, and a passive community.

At last an example will be made, at last the party charged will feel that justice, though slow, is sure—that this court, as far as they can give their sanction, will have it to be understood, that the members of this bar are not only to be honest, but, like Cæsar's wife, above suspicion.

The respondent, as well as his counsel, have touched upon a variety of topics not connected with the merits of this investigation, at one time arraigning the conduct of magistrates as oppressive and vindictive, and on that account claiming the protection of your honours, at another time considerations of domestic affliction have been thrown in to excite sympathy and compassion, as if this Court could be moved from the course which the facts, and their duty, prescribe. And yet, although indulgence, sympathy, pity, have been all invoked in behalf of Mr. Niven, we have witnessed with how much apparent confidence he has relied upon his unspotted purity—how fervently he has spoken of the testimony of a good conscience, and the value of reputation. He has, indeed, given a striking illustration of the truth, that " hypocrisy is the tribute which vice pays to virtue." Honour, conscience, and principle have been chimed from the beginning to the ending of his appeals, and, if the facts did not belie his tongue, he might find credit for some portion of honourable sentiment.

The counsel, in their remarks on the affidavits, and Mr. Niven himself, in the fulness of his ire, against the police magistrates, have affected great alarm, least the public liberties should be altogether broken down; they see, or think they see, imminent dangers to the laws of the land, in the affidavits which have been taken by the police officers—in the presentment of the grand jury, and the proceedings by the court against their client.

How? where? why should the magistrates close their ears to complaints against a lawyer, if such complaints deserved redress? Why should not a grand jury proceed with as much vigour against one offender as another? I am not aware, that the members of the bar claim greater privileges than other men, when morals become the subject of inquiry. The truth is, if it please the court, that oppression is the theme on which desperate men delight to dwell. The unfortunate, and the guilty, exercise the glorious privilege of exclaiming oppression! oppression! oppression! In their eyes every prison is a *monument* of its horrors—every court a *memento* of cruelty—every judge the instrument of injustice, and every jury the creature of exaction. In boyhood this dire oppression stings the breech of the truant, when the ferrule of the master is applied, and, in manhood, it throttles the thief, by the arm of the law. The vagabond, no longer feasting on the refuse of the kitchen, snatched from delicious slumbers in sunshine and filth—constrained by the *iron* rod of oppression, within the walls of a prison, curses and disdains oppression, in the oakum which he picks—the Cyprian of Bancker St. cut off from the midnight revel—the inspiring joys of the fiddle and the dance, while sipping the cooling beverage of her tyrant the turnkey, scolds, frets, and bears it. The pick-axe, and the chain of the wheelbarrow-convict, jingle a morning and evening lamentation over the horrors of oppression; they rattle vengeance against the bolts and bars of penitentiary persecution. At every term of the criminal court, the *highwayman*, the *forger*, the *thief*, solemnly protest against it as a *hellish* invasion of the rights of man.

It would be strange if the party arraigned did not avail himself of the privilege exercised from time immemorial, by all offending against the law, and in danger of punishment.

Cases have been stated, and the practice of Roman advocates adduced to justify the conduct of Mr. Niven. It is unnecessary to refer to the example of Roman lawyers, if any weight could be derived from the example of a corrupt period; nor will the annals of English jurisprudence shed light upon the question now depending. What though houses and lands were received by the Roman lawyers—what though large fees were retained by English barristers as a *quiddam honorarium*, when no service was rendered. If these cases would apply here, are we to decide questions of morals, and of propriety, by precedents from Roman and English authority, when we have lights of our own brighter than antiquity could boast—lights of reason and justice which require no aid from Roman usages, or the practice of English courts?

The acts complained of are acts of dishonesty, gross, palpable *dishonesty*—which, if committed by any individual, whatever might be his station or profession, ought to render him infamous for ever. The counsel mistake, if they suppose, that we consider the offence of their client to consist in the mere taking of articles of furniture, clothing, and watches, as fees. We go further. We say, that he has not only taken articles of this kind, but that he acquired the possession by fraudulent means, by representations of the basest character, by contrivances of the blackest description.

(*Here the counsel examined the affidavits, and detailed the conduct of Mr. Niven as to the manner he obtained orders for the property of the prisoners.*)

It is objected, that the testimony of the prisoners ought not to be received to establish the facts against the respondent But are we not to take their declarations as to facts which they alone are competent to establish ? If some, who are said by the counsel to be thieves and prostitutes, assail the integrity of their client, have not others of the like character been introduced by Niven himself, to establish his morals ? Has he not resorted to the aid of reputed and imprisoned thieves, to prove his reputation to be good ?

Entrenched as he thinks himself by affidavits exculpatory and accusatory, the proofs he has made establish guilt—they make some points certain, which were doubtful before—surrounded as he is by damning facts, like the scorpion within a circle of fire, he stings himself to death.

Let us proceed to an examination of the affidavits, and without dwelling long upon the prominent facts, we will soon *fix* the value of his professional merits, and his character as a man. I would not be fastidious in a case of this nature ; on the contrary, before a member of the bar is disbarred for malpractice, I would require evidence—strong evidence of the facts alleged against him, not resting upon refined notions of professional delicacy, because some men may be more scrupulous than others, without having better claims to reputation.

One charge and it is a material one, which is made out by three witnesses, Stivers, Charley, and Kerland, uncontradicted by the affidavits of Niven, in my view is sufficient to decide the merits of this case.

By the affidavits of these three witnesses, they were induced to employ Niven, partly by the solicitations of his *stool pigeons* Davis and Milligan, and more particularly the extraordinary fabrications of Niven himself; at one time to one unfortunate prisoner representing that he Niven had great influence with the police, to another, that if he did not give him a fee, the state prison would be his doom, and to a third that the police would get all the money and property he possessed if he refused to employ him as his counsel.

Intimidated by such methods, and influenced by the creatures of

Niven within the gates of bridewell, he succeeds in obtaining a bedstead, a watch, a table from one ; money and clothing from the other two.

(*The counsel read extracts from the affidavits of Kerland, Charley and Stivers, and commented on them, and the exculpatory affidavits.*)

Now, here we find a member of the bar who has sworn to demean himself honestly in the discharge of his duty—wilfully and knowingly committing the vilest falsehood, to induce the prisoners to employ him—holding up the magistrates as influenced by the most wicked motives, and colleaguing with other prisoners to secure his prey.

(*Here the affidavits were again referred to, and commented on.*)

The duty of the advocate is sometimes an unpleasant one, he is not to shun what may be within the pale of his professional calling ; and it is with pride and pleasure I say, that this bar furnishes many instances of the most intrepid discharge of duty, in cases of palpable guilt, without the least imputation resting on the counsel. But, was it ever heard ? Is it ever to be tolerated, that a member of the profession shall hunt up the acknowledged and confessed felon, that he shall way-lay the doors of the prison—that he shall inveigle—terrify—deceive—possess himself of property when no service could be rendered—frighten his miserable victim when he cannot coax him to deliver his little property. I ask, is this conduct to be justified ? Is this not proved to be the course pursued by Niven? has he contradicted it by his own sweeping affidavits ?

Stivers confessed his guilt on his examination at the police office—he avowed his guilt to Niven in the bridewell. Niven swears, that Stivers told him he was guilty and was to be made a witness against others. But Niven ascertains, that he has some furniture, and a watch ; he is not content until he obtains an order on the wife of the prisoner to deliver her bedstead, and table, &c. This order was obtained by the vilest contrivances.

(*The counsel again refers to the affidavit.*)

But the counsel insist, that no credit attaches to the affidavit of Stivers ! Why ? Because, say they, he made another and subsequent affidavit contradicting the matter stated in the first. It is true, that Stivers, unable to read or write, did swear to a second affidavit ! Here, again, is another fact of extraordinary depravity on the part of Niven. Stivers declares, that he never meant to contradict his first statement, that if the affidavit procured by Niven did contradict it—that then it had never been read correctly to him. But Niven swears that he read it twice to Stivers, and his brother Henry Niven

"*Sequitur que patrem non passibus æquis.*"

deposes that he was present when it was read twice distinctly in the hearing of Stivers What is the character of this second affidavit from circumstances which cannot lie ? It is the *only* one taken in the handwriting of Niven ; the other affidavits are drawn by his counsel ; his own affidavits are not in his own handwriting ; and yet an affidavit which Niven considered so vitally important to his case, concerning facts which had, already been the subject of a presentment by a grand jury: this affidavit of Stivers, obtained by Niven, is not taken before, or by a respectable *counsel*, or a judge, or notary, or any official person, but by Niven himself, read in the presence of Niven's brother, in a corner of the Judges Chambers who subscribed the jurat, but who was not requested to read it to the party deposing, nor to be present when read by Niven.

Again ; does not this surreptitious affidavit bear evident marks upon the face of it, to put down the allegation that it was twice distinctly read to Stivers before he deposed ?

If read with so much care, if examined with such caution, it is reasonable to suppose, that the sense would be expressed with sufficient clearness before it was sworn to. But examine the affidavit itself—the original words written with ink—which state, that the deposition first made by Stivers, was taken under the direction of Stivers himself, are altered in pencil, in the handwriting of Niven, so as to make the sense altogether different.

(*Here the affidavit was read, and the alteration particularly pointed out.*)

Now, one of two predicaments; if the affidavit, as originally drawn, and "twice distinctly read," was true, then how dare Niven falsify it by the alteration ? If it was not true, as originally drawn, what validity can there be in the oath of Niven, and his brother, when they depose to the caution with which it was drawn, read, and sworn to.

Mr. Niven here interrupted the counsel, stating, that this was a malicious insinuation, and Mr. Bogardus insisted, that the alteration ought to have been pointed out before.

Judge Irving. The gentleman is arguing upon the face of the affidavit. you will be heard in due time.

Mr. Niven again interrupts.

Judge Irving. It is impossible to go through with such an investigation without something disagreeable. The interruption of counsel is very improper.

Maxwell. It is unfortunate that some men, when hard pressed, affect passion, and too often betray themselves by their own babbling.

(*Here the counsel particularly examined the facts set forth in the affidavits of Kerland and Charley, and compared them with the allegations in the exculpatory affidavits*)

One of the counsel in endeavouring to destroy the credit of Charley, asked the court in a very triumphant manner, whether it could be believed that after Niven had told Charley, that "he was guilty as all hell, and all hell could not save him," that Charley would be so stupified as to give Niven $5 as a fee. But let me ask with greater confidence, did not Niven induce Stivers **who acknowledged his guilt, and who had no defence to make,** to

deliver as a fee, articles of furniture ? and does not Niven in his own affidavit admit that he received $5 from this very Charley.
(*Here he reads the affidavit.*)

The learned counsel lament the condition of their client, that he has not the benefit of a trial by jury. Ought he not rather to rejoice that this proceeding enables him to introduce his own oath in his defence ? He has been obliged to resort to it, but it is a refuge which cannot, which ought not to prove impregnable, did he stand fully acquitted by his own affidavits.

A sensible and celebrated writer in his essay on oaths, (Beccaria on crimes and punishments) has illustrated the danger of this mode of defence. " There is a palpable contradiction between the laws and the natural sentiments of mankind in the case of oaths, which are administered to a criminal to make him speak the truth, when the contrary is his greatest interest ; as if a man could think himself obliged to contribute to his own destruction, and as if when interest speaks, religion was not generally silent, religion which in all ages hath, of all other things been most commonly abused." "The motives which religion opposes to the fear of impending evil and love of life are too weak, as they are too distant to make any impression on the senses." " I appeal to every judge," he continues, " whether he has ever known that an oath alone has brought truth from the lips of a criminal ; and reason tells us it must be so, for all laws are useless, and in consequence destructive which contradict the natural feelings of mankind."

It is contended that the affidavit of Niven is of equal force with the affidavit of each of the complainants taken *singly*. and that in the deciding of this matter, the court must take up each affidavit unconnected with the charges in the others, and decide upon the merits of each affidavit, as if it stood unconnected with any other containing similar charges. Not so if it please the court. The whole case is to be viewed, the perfect whole is to be considered, the parts are to be fitted and compared; they show a system of profligiacy which does not, cannot appear without an examination of the whole.

(*Here the counsel referred to the several affidavits.*)

Would the counsel pronounce upon the flavour of the fruit by a single leaf from the tree ? judge of the deformity, the magnitude of the animal by a single hair from its tail ? or from the disjointed member of a skeleton delineate the full and perfect man ?

A certificate from a number of the members of the bar, has been read to prove the character of Niven. How much attention that certificate deserves, the court must decide. I must confess, that I was not a little surprised to see how much importance was given to a certificate which proves nothing. Some of the gentlemen whose names have been read, I know would disdain to certify any thing but the truth; they have certified in substance, that Niven has never cheated them; that is the amount of it, and nothing more. Do they speak of character ? Do they give the legal evidence of reputation ? No, because they could give no other than that contained in the presentment of the grand jury.

Are the gentlemen indeed of that character,

" That palter with us in a double sense,
That keep the word of promise to the ear,
And break it to our hope."

I trust not. They speak of their transactions with Mr. Niven exclusively; and because they have been so fortunate as to escape the toils of their client, is he therefore honest since he has left them uninjured ? Has no other felt the effects of his injustice ? Will they certify that there is no poison in the bite of the rattle snake since they have never suffered by its fangs ? Is there no fierceness in the wolf, or rapacity in the shark, because they may have escaped the one and avoided the other ?

But whatever objection may exist as to the credibility of Stivers, Charley, and Kerland, how will Mr. Niven answer the charges contained in the other affidavits, charges of so serious a character as to require the most satisfactory explanation.

(*The counsel then went into an examination of the other affidavits in detail, which is omitted here.*)

The affidavit of Ellen Griffin is fortified by the oath of Collins, an unimpeachable witness ; this woman is brought before the magistrate, convicted under the act, and sentenced to the penitentiary for six months ; what service could Mr. Niven or any other professional man render her ? Yet he promises to aid her, and succeeds in obtaining possession of her clothing. She serves her time out; not having received any assistance from her lawyer, she reclaims the garments which Niven holds as security for his fee. Did he not know she was convicted as a prostitute ? Did he not know that he could render her no service ? Was it not clear that the wretched woman was entitled to a restitution ? In answer to this charge, he talks about the bill of rights, the constitution of the state, and the invasion of civil rights. But does he deny the fact ? No he admits that he received her property, and that he has possession of it still ; he contends too, that he is honestly entitled to retain it, as his *quiddam honorarium.* Honorable advocate ! disinterested man ! lofty member of the bar ! who at one moment with vivacious intellect, scans the fundamental principles of constitutional liberty, and at the next explores with sagacious prudence the rocks and quicksands, covered by the statute against false pretences ; who at one instant soars into the regions of civil and political liberty, fired with wrath at the violation of *private* rights, and now dives amid the gew gaws of a prostitutes band box, discussing with legal *acumen* the parapharnalia appertaining to the mysteries of the Hook, *battening* on the stench of foul linen, through all its varieties, from the smock that covered, up to the ruffled rag which served to adorn the nakedness of his client ! !

The affidavit of Davenport discloses another disgraceful transaction, too disgraceful for the vilest tipstaff.

(*Here the counsel read the facts from Davenport's affidavit.*)
Davenport is on the limits, at the suit of Nivens' client. The law had effected all which could be effected by the attorney in the suit. His client could require no more, and no honest, honourable lawyer would suffer an intimation, that after the discharge of his legitimate functions, he was to be employed as the instrument to induce an escape, and the spy and the witness to prove it. This would indeed be too much for any man, but it was a trifle to this honourable attorney ; he engages in it—he lays his plan—he cajoles his victim—he entices him off the limits—he makes his brother a *particeps criminis*—he causes the bail to be prosecuted for an escape—he appears as witness himself, and the jury find a verdict for the defendant?

Do you doubt the truth of Davenport's statement? not surely because Niven and his brother swear there was no plan of this kind contrived! for Mr Jennings a respectable man deposes, that he heard Niven boast publicly, that " he had laid a plan to catch Davenport off the limits, and gloried in having succeeded."

Davenport himself stands before the court, supported by three respectable men, as a witness entitled to unquestioned veracity.
(*Mr Maxwell reads the affidavits again in the case of Cohenhoven.*)
Couenhoven deposits money with his lawyer Mr. Niven, to discharge a judgment obtained against him; (*he refers to the affidavit and conversation,*) This money amounted to about $40. Niven promises to apply to discharge the claim against his client. Instead of doing so he pockets the money, allows two suits to be commenced against the bail, and when called upon by Covenhoven to refund the amount, he has the effrontery to bring in a bill, in which the costs of the two suits occasioned by his own malpractice and breach of trust form the principal items. But even admitting that Covenhoven was indebted to his attorney Niven in a much larger sum, by what rule of morals, or of law, can he justify the deceit practised and attempted to be defended?

Is it necessary, to say one word, in relation to the affidavit of Robert Lattimore? this affidavit which they have not answered, and which they could not, dare not meet, except by the technical objection, that an indictment had been preferred on the charges contained in that affidavit on which the defendant was acquitted. Not on the merits, as has been stated, but on a variance between a paper set out in the indictment, the proof offered.

(*Here the counsel was about to read from the report of the case, but the court thought it was inconsistent with their former decision.*)

I say nothing of the affidavit of Shoemaker, put that out of the case, and enough, too much, remains before the court. The acquittal in the case of Lattimore is no protection here, and no just complaint can be made that the matters charged are of a long date, and too stale to deserve the serious notice of your honours. I apprehend that the court will adopt the rule as established by lord Mansfield in the case of Brounsall, an attorney, 2 Cowper 829.

It was an application by the magistrates of the county to strike Brounsall off the roll of attornies, he having been convicted of stealing a guinea. Lord Mansfield said, "this application is not in the nature of a second trial or a new punishment. But the question is, whether after the conduct of this man, it is proper that he should continue a member of the profession which should stand free from all suspicion." And on a subsequent day, lord Mansfield said, "we have consulted the judges upon this case, and they are unanimously of opinion, that the defendant having been burnt in the hand is no objection to his being struck off the roll; and it is on this principle, that he is an unfit person to practice as an attorney. It is not by way of punishment; but the court in such cases exercise its discretion, whether a man whom they have formerly admitted, is a proper person to be continued on the roll or not." Cowp. 829.

In the case of the king against Southerton, 6 Eart. 142, lord Ellenborough after giving judgment in favour of the defendant who had been indicted for sending a threatning letter, said, "Enough appeared to the court to satisfy them, that the defendant was a very improper person to remain as an attorney on the rolls of the court." His name was afterwards accordingly struck off the roll.

The cases cited on a former occasion must be in the recollection of the court and I need not dwell upon what acts constitute an offence sufficiently criminal to degrade a member of the profession. The good sense and intelligence of your honours must decide that without reference to authorities.

But I must notice one position assumed by the counsel, they say that if their client be guilty of the matters charged in the affidavits, let him be punished by a regular proceeding by indictment. I answer that an offence of this nature committed by an attorney is not punishable at common law; this was decided by judge Yates, on the trial of the indictment preferred by Lattimore on an objection taken by the defendant.

The proper, the only mode of reaching him, is by this proceeding, and no other has been provided by the law.

As to the suggestion that if any offence is proved against Mr. Niven, it is proved against him as counsel, and not as an attorney; the court will find no difficulty in this; attornies and counsellors are admitted and entered on the rolls as such, the characters of both are united in the person of the respondent, and he is amenable to this forum in both capacities; if he is unworthy as a counsellor, he is equally so as an attorney. My learned friend, says, that this court ought not to listen to the disclosures made by clients against their counsel; that it is the privilege of the counsel to insist upon secrecy. I contend that counsel have no such right, it would be a monstrous inversion of justice. And this very point was decided by judge Yates in the case alluded to, to be untenable, of which the gentleman who raised it, cannot be ignorant.

I am aware that much has been said, perhaps too much, in the address of counsel, but the nature of this case seemed to require it.

From a deliberate and unimpasioned view of the conduct of this individual, as disclosed in the affidavits; from the course too which he has pursued during this investigation, I do not hesitate to declare my conviction, that he ought no longer to be honoured by a station at this bar, I consider him as a professional monster, swelling into *magnitude*, amid damps and darkness, whose aliment has been drawn not from his condition as a member of the profession in the ligitimate exercise of his vocation, not from the discharge of duties, the privilege as well as the protection of the accused. No, his life and being had been sustained, and invigorated by the injustice which he has inflicted upon misfortune, by moral wounds cankered and inflamed by his fraud, by the tears and misery which his avarice and artifice have aggravated and insulted. The rankness of moral turpitude springing up in the productive soil of the prison and the bagnio has acquired increased vigour from the sunshine of his favour, and I am compelled to add, deserves some protection from the boldness, the impunity of of his example Men are wicked from temptation, from habitudes of crime. But where did the older offender or the tyranic iniquity until now disclaim altogether the obligations of virtue. This man claims a distinguished place on the calendar, he disdains the petit larceny infirmity incident to weak minds, that confesses guilt, and prays the mercy of the court. Even here undone a load of guilt *onerous* enough to stagger, to crush the firmest reputation of a united, nay, of the universal bar. Here under the concentrated light of multiplied proofs, one ray of which ought to wither, and consume the guilty object, even here he has asserted the native impudence of his character. For he would practice, he would impose upon this court, by wishing them to mistake the effrontery of detected fraud, for the confidence of injured innocence; he assails the motives and character of men, far beyond the reach of his feeble malice, vainly hoping to find a colour for his own misconduct. If I mistake not, he thinks that a false compassion, or a forgiving temper, or perhaps the fear of his potent anger will alleviate, if it shall not avert punishment.

I for one in the name of this bar, do most solemnly protest against his being continued within the pale of a profession designed for the accomplishment of dignified objects, by the talents and industry of honourable advocates.

The public has long since demanded his expulsion, the bar has been too long disgraced by his offences, let sentence be pronounced against him, let the condemnation of professional death be inflicted, if it be severe, it will at least be merited, it will be just.

Mr. Wilkins began by observing, that little was left for him to say by the counsel who preceded him; but some few observations it was his duty to make, in reprehension of conduct degrading to the profession, immoral and dangerous in its tendency as regards public policy and justice. My friend, Mr. Anthon, has stated it as a matter of defence, that his client was acting as a counsellor, and, therefore, not liable to the same animadversion or discipline as if he had been acting merely as an attorney; and for this he adduces certain instances from England which have no application to this case. Counsellors cannot be attornies in England, and are admitted in quite different form. The only question there, has been touching the mode in which the one and the other was to be silenced and restrained. With respect to the counsellor, he is disrobed or disbarred; the attorney is struck out of the roll of the attornies of the court. Here they act in both capacities, and the principal duty of the court is to prevent them from committing crimes or misdemeanors, under its leave and license. When they find their licence abused, and the public suffer by it, not to withdraw that licence would be to sanction the abuses. The counsel, as well as the attorney, signs the roll of the court, and that roll is the evidence of his honesty and sufficiency. When the court can no longer conscientiously certify to the public for the morality of its officer, it revokes the letter of credit it has given by the simple process of striking his name out of the roll of counsellors, and of attorneys, and will, at all events, protect the public, and chasten the profession by silencing the faithless counsellor, and disqualifying the delinquent attorney. We find, that such have been not only stricken off, but summarily fined and imprisoned, and even ordered into the pillory. Without some such extraordinary powers a court would be placed in the delicate and difficult situation of responsibility without authority, and, if once deceived by a certificate, a thing in many cases too easily procured, the judges must shut their eyes, and fold their arms, whilst their officer, under their express authority, plunders the community, and brings the law and its ministers into condign disgrace. It was, therefore, a forlorn defence, and such as one of Mr. Anthon's talents would not have resorted to, had any better been within his reach.

As to Mr. Bogardus, however sound he may be upon other subjects, he was like one crazy upon this; unless it was, that seeing nothing in the evidence that could justify his client, he determined to raise up a smoke, and carry the war, by right or by wrong, into some other quarter. He, therefore, set up a cry of thieves, felons, prostitutes, forgers and receivers, perjuries, conspiracies and oppressions. After railing against the witnesses, he falls upon the magistrates, and represents them as bad men and conspirators, because they issued a sub,œna to a person who testified to the fraud, if not perjury of one whose dangerous threats were calculated to inspire witnesses with terror, and make them think themselves unsafe if they appeared without such process. The only witness, however, that did receive a subpœna, was most strictly a witness for the people. And credit, not censure, is due to the police, for the law has constituted them guardians of the public safety, and made it their duty to be alert in bringing iniquity to light, and issuing process to witnesses who are necessary to justice. Why else do they sit there?

The next attack was on the grand jury. They were ship masters and merchants, and so forth, and what then? Had that anything to do with Mr. Niven's degrading, and foul practices? They were the grand jury of the county, charged on their oaths to inform the court of all offences, and dilligently for that purpose to inquire into all violations of the law. It was peculiarly their province to inquire into abuses in the presence of the court; and if they found that a lawyer had been guilty of mal-practices were they to stand appalled, and suffer the evil to proceed. Any body may make this denunciation or presentment as a friend to to the court; but it is the peculiar province and duty of the grand jury, and all that has been said of the difference between presenting persons, and presenting things, is without any foundation in law, or common sense. The court, however, have indulged the party by leaving this presentment out of their consideration, and proceeding upon the evidence independently, and exclusively of it: he cannot, therefore, complain with any show of reason. It cannot be, that a lawyer has a privilege to break the laws, or violate his oath of office, and that there shall be no inquiry. Though the offences charged upon this man are private frauds, and not indictable, yet if a counsellor will so far degrade himself as to go into your bridewell to solicit business, put the wretches in false terror, hook in with prostitutes, and extort money—if he will take the clothes of these rogues, vagabonds, and prostitutes, by the way of fees, or pledges for fees, is he to continue a member of a profession which, however noble and elevated, when exercised with purity and honour, is fearful and hideous when it is made the road to such vile gains.

The defence shows more than the accusation, the character of the unhappy man. He is at war with all authority; grand jurors, justices, witnesses, his own clients in and out of bridewell, gaoler, turnkeys, and constables, all are in a conspiracy to persecute him for defending the constitution and the people's rights. And, finally, he falls upon me. Upon me who certainly never did conspire against him. I have never had any thing to do with him. The affidavits were not prepared by me. I first saw them the very day that I came here, when they were shown to me in Mr. Skaats's room as a matter of curiosity. The court, and these very marble walls, were also denounced, and I was astonished, that in so many words, there was not one that bore the sound of justification or excuse.

One topic touched my sense. The consequences of the sentence to his wife and children. There I was touched with sorrow. But this must be the case with every man brought to the bar of justice. And the court are bound by their duty and their oaths, by their sacred obligations, both to God and man, to administer law, and do justice to the community. The sentence that punishes guilt, and protects the public, is not their sentence, to pass, or to withhold at pleasure, and the audacity of the offender is a reason the more that he should be humbled.

It is said that he is accused by thieves, and forgers, and prostitutes, and vagabonds. It may be so, but why put himself in the power of such? If indeed the matters stood at all in doubt and there was no other testimony, the argument might have its weight. But I shall show that there is no doubt; and that what those thieves have sworn is intrinsically true, and that their testimony is fully supported. In vain then is all this outcry of perjury, subornation, and conspiracy. If I can show from unimpeached testimony, that both Mr. Niven and his brother have deliberately sworn, what they knew was not true, the whole of their defence falls at once to the earth. And I shall show that in spite of the host of affidavits and oaths so multiplied, the whole ground is not covered, and that they have admitted enough to convict this member of the bar, of practices unworthy of his degree

I shall not toil through the whole labyrinth. I have made extracts from the affidavits of Stivers and the answer to it, which may serve the turn. Stivers was arrested for stealing soap or soap fat, from Mr. Colgate. He confessed. Before god and my country he says I have no defence. But whilst in jail he meets with the whale's pilot, Mr. Davis, who tells him that he must employ Mr. Niven the honestest and most magnanimous counsel at the bar. He takes him up just as he has confessed his sins, and gone so far towards forgiveness. He advises him against the fallacy and folly of confession. He represents Mr. Colgate and the police as in a faithless league against him, and offers to defend him in spite of his confessions. He terrifies him till he sheds tears, and Davis urges on the crisis, till at length in his paroxysm he begs of this kind protector of the injured, to take all he had his watch, his gun, his table, and his bedstead, and save him from the conspirators. Did ever lawyer so degrade himself? Did ever honest man receive such reward for such iniquity?

Compare this with the conduct of any honourable member of the profession. What would such an one do in such a case? tell the repentant sinner who had already obtained the honest promise of the community, which has never been forfeited to any prisoner to retract what he had acknowledged, to jeopardize himself anew, and provoke the arm of justice by redoubling his guilt. Would he league with such a comrade as that Davis, the one to prompt and persuade the wretched, the other to take the booty? It appears that this prisoner being discharged by the interference of Mr. Boardman, asks for his property, of which one article only is restored. But he some how contrives to get the mark of that illiterate man to an affidavit directly contradicting what he had positively sworn before. This was not perjury in Stivers, because Stivers was deceived. Was it perjury in Mr. Niven? perhaps not in judgment of the law, because he did not make the oath himself, but by whatever name it may be known on earth, in heaven, it is recorded for what it truly is. He knew that the day before he had made an affidavit in a quite opposite sense, that it lay upon the table; yet he gets him to swear or set his mark to this, which the fact itself shows that he did not understand. There is but one way of solving this strange mystery; and that is by supposing that some nefarious juggling was practiced upon this ignorant man. He might be thief or rogue, or what you will, but there is only one that could have the effrontery to venture on such a desperate course. If your honour was to take an affidavit under such circumstances with knowledge of its contents, would you not be impeached; and could it be possible that an affidavit containing such a story, could be twice distinctly read in your presence and you not mark it? And why, *twice* distinctly read to him? Does not that *twice* argue deception and trick? Is it not in its very nature and character a badge of fraud? Was this affidavit voluntary and spontaneous? It appears not. It is drawn up by Mr. Niven himself; and however it was managed, the man no sooner hears it represented that he had made an affidavit of such a tendency, than he expresses his surprise, comes into court and swears that if he has sworn to any such thing it was not what was read to him, or that he did not understand it. If this be not subornation what then is it? What would a candid upright man have done if his story had been true? He would have taken the witness into the presence of a judge, and prayed that in his presence and hearing, the whole contents might be not twice but once distinctly read to him. But no, and your honour was thus induced to swear him generally, and of course to the truth of his deposition without being informed in any manner of its peculiar nature. And all I have now to say upon it is, that if this man's guilt was great before it is doubled by this deed.

The next witness is poor Kerland. He was taken up, because he happened to be found in a house where counterfeit money was discovered. This man was not convicted, and is certainly a competent witness. He was in no danger whatever, and apprehended none till Mr. Davis or some of this virtuous fraternity, who patronized Mr. Niven, and from whom he has stooped to ask for a character, and who are like himself persecuted by grand juries, and justices and jailors, tell him he must employ this generous advocate of the oppressed, else there is no salvation for him. The lawyer assures him he has great interest with the police. If he had, that indeed would be some impeachment of the police, but it does not appear; or if it was so, he makes a strange return for their favour, by all this rank abuse. No! But it answered his purpose to say so, in order to extort the poor man's money. Without me and my interest you must go to the state prison. The terrified wretch is drawn in to give five dollars with a promise of ten on a future day. And for collateral security his deliverer takes his trunk of clothes, which he has never returned to him. Are these practices becoming of a counsellor at law? to go into the bridewell and frighten poor prisoners out of their clothes! and shall one so degraded stand up in the face of a court, affecting such extravagant strains of noble indignation and muck honour, and profess himself the champion of rights and an avengor of wrongs, the maintainer of the constitution and the bill of rights. Is it not past all comprehension? Has he no sense, no feeling of what is right or wrong?

The next is Charley. Poor Charley's crime was not great, taken in its extent. He bought three razors for three shillings. Mr. Niven is presented to him by Davis, or some other of his friends at court, and gets an order for his watch on the police. The court must have had some difficulty in persuading themselves that this man was an object of conviction or punishment, and he was, indeed, accordingly acquitted. But Mr. Niven, not getting the watch, frightens him till he sells his gun, and pays him the five dollars. And, that he afterwards got, and kept the watch, he does not deny. Can it be possible, that this court would so far sink and degrade the profession in the estimation of the community, as to pronounce this conduct justifiable? If so, and counsel are tolerated in such acts, where is this licenciousness to stop? Will they be authorized to perpetrate robberies or rapes?

Mr. Couhenhoven's business is more complicated, and I shall only notice it to show, that Mr. Niven, and his brother, are positively contradicted in a story which, indeed, required no contradiction; for it was, in itself, improbable and unnatural. If this be so, if they have sworn false in this matter, it reflects back upon all their evidence, and Stivers's last affidavit, as well as his first, stands confirmed, and the defence made by Mr. Niven is the blackest part of his whole history. In vain are his abusive terms. In vain when he takes the money placed in his hands, and applies it to his own use, and suffers himself to be sued, and charges the costs of that delinquency to his client, it is in vain to answer, it was a damned rascal. The money was due by the judgment of a court. The lawyer takes it upon his responsibility, and it is delivered in that confidence which the office of a counsellor on the rolls of the court inspires, for, on the credit of the court, the individual is trusted. He was bound to apply it to that judgment. It was a base and flagrant breach of trust to Couherrhoven, a fraud upon Stivers, and an indignity to the courts, whose license was abused to purposes so villainous.

As to Shoemaker, we are told that he was a mayor, a lawyer, a broker, a—and perhaps an insolvent or a pauper. His crime was, however, that of sleeping in a lawyer's office, begging for bread, and, perhaps, writing very laboriously to pay for it. It is not, however, what he was, but what Mr. Niven did, that is the question before this court. Go bail for him, I shall have the bail reduced, let him run away, and I will apply to the exchequer for a remission. This was not done, the man is called to take his trial, Mr. Niven goes up and speaks to him, and he immediately pleads guilty, and is sent to the penitentiary. He may have done nothing wrong in this, but why advise Stivers, who had confessed, and was forgiven, to revoke his confession, and advise this man to plead guilty, who had not confessed: unless that [illegible] had no watch, nor furniture, nor clothes, to give or pledge. Why did he desire that nothing should be said about it, unless he felt he had done something that required concealment.

Ellen Griffin was a prostitute! This state of being was punishment enough for all her sins. But she was convicted, and sent to the penitentiary. Up steps the champion of the constitution, and gives her hopes of pardon, tells her the bill of rights must be looked into. What a picture is here of human degradation, to see this proud upholder of the constitution seeking for the bill of rights amongst the pettycoats, stockings, and shifts, and all the tattered, tawdry decorations of her miserable profession! What right had he to take these things for the obtaining of her pardon? Is it thus that the delicate attribute of pardoning is to be sported with and profaned? Is it thus that the administration of law and justice is to be held forth to the ignorant? What respect can they have for courts, or officers of courts or for the law, if one who claims a title to faith and credit, by virtue of the record of a court, gives practical lessons of such vile debasement? yet this is the high and lofty character that cannot endure to have his unsullied honour touched. It is attempted to give some countenance to this, by saying, that the lawyers in the western parts take produce and cattle for their fees. I do not see why they should not accept a present of a pair of oxen, or a horse, or any produce which their client chooses to offer them; but, I trust, when they do so, that they take nothing but fair fees for honourable offices. Is that a reason that this his conduct should be tolerated? Can this tribunal look on these proceedings without horror? I certainly cannot. I shudder when I think, that I must, to get my livelihood, stand up in the ranks with such a being. I had much to say of Mrs. Holman's case, but I forbear. The court have excluded this matter from discussion. I never choose to contend with the court, and when it has decided any point, I know that submission is my duty.

I shall now show the falsehood of both brothers as to the affair of Davenport. And in the first place, that he is worthy of credit is sworn by two upright and disinterested witnesses. There was a controversy between the lawyer and the client, Mr. Niven insists that he paid him for his beef, with counsel about lands and lord knows what. A referee was appointed, and the lawyer invites him to go with him to the referee, and they go arm in arm to the office of Mr. M'Donald the referee. He coaxes him to Dey-Street, when he detains him till he can look about a horse and chair, at Dawson's stables. But the other tells him they have moved from that. Never mind there will be some one there. But I am off the limits—is that safe? oh yes you are quite safe when you are with me. Mr. Niven's brother who was anxious to hear Goodwin's trial summed up, happens to straggle to that spot and is posted in readiness to catch him there, and instantly of his own head and imagination, issues the process in the name of this very attorney, who sues that action. And all this without his assent or even his knowledge. This very attorney on the record goes afterwards to Mr. Jennings, and boasts to him, that he had fixed one devil off the limits, that he gloried in it, and moreover that his name was Davenport. There is much bold reliance upon the contradiction given to this story by both Mr. Niven and his brother. And the hacknied phrase " it is positively denied, is much relied upon. I know that it is positively denied," but denied or not I say that it is positively true, and that denied was the parting word of the witnesses expiring credit. If these two brothers are both so deliberately forsworn, what remains behind. And how shall it be said, that this man is not guilty of all and of much more than he was charged with, bad as that was?

But his character is supported—By whom? By two witnesses! Who are they? Mr. Wood, forsooth, and Mr. Bell! Let us look into this and see whether their friendly recommendation is not of itself enough to throw him over the bar of this court. It is a dispensation of providence that guilt betrays itself. Might I not here go upon a rough guess and using the arguments of Mr. Niven's counsel, say they were inmates of bridewell, rogues of course, and vagabonds. Mr. Niven to be sure draws up long and prolix affidavits for them, in which he represents himself almost a saint, bestowing upon himself almost all the christian virtues, and arraignes the officers of justice of every mortal crime. He joins with these prisoners in raising up sedition against their keeper and all his deputies : and must the officers of the police see this, know this, that corruption is more corrupted, that the prison is agitated, and order set at defiance and not dare to take any measures to prevent it?

Last in order comes what I am most sorry to see is the certificate of what is called " the bar," I cannot deny that there are there some names of high respectability. I sincerely regret that their credit was not reserved to grace and countenance a worthier object and a better cause. Perhaps by this time they are sorry likewise. I will impute to none of those gentlemen any but good motives; and I hope, that it may be a caution hereafter to good nature to be upon its guard ; and prevent this facility in signing whatever is presented, or whether it grows out of our social state, or whether it is the fashion of the times, it is most sure, that there is nothing now a days in the shape of a petition or certificate to which signatures may not be had, as long as they are to have no obligation upon the signer. Abuses however, will in due time cure themselves, and good men once surprised will, it is hoped, be so no more. But what does this certificate so pompously displayed amount to? It sheds one solitary ray of light upon this dark picture, enough to expose to fuller view the appalling traces of hypocrisy and art. Mr. Niven had not cheated any of these gentlemen in the course of his practice with them! Be it so: Perhaps he never had it in his power. The intelligent and exprienced were not his marks: these he could not practice on, he preyed upon the indigent and the wretched. Those he could terrify and mould to his will, they were powerless, and he feared no resistance nor recrimination from them. He could turn a deaf ear to their remonstrance, put them out of his doors, and bid them go to hell. Turpin the highwayman was a notorious robber, he was tried, condemned, and hanged for robbery: yet he could no doubt have obtained the signatures of ten thousand Englishmen to a certificate or to an affidavit, that he never robbed them! The duty assigned to me by this honourable court, was to examine into the evidence, th t duty I have now discharged. There was room enough for more display of elocution in speaking of that man and of his acts: But I pity him and feel for his family, and would have had more pleasure in restoring him to his character, could I have done it with honesty. My office has been that of an humble minister in this temple of justice. It is done. I have bound the victim, let the court perform the sacrifice

Mr. Niven, after Mr. Wilkins had concluded, addressed the court. He pledged himself to come out clear of the charges made against him by this combination of his enemies, but prayed the aid of his counsel to reply in his stead, to the very studied speech of one man, and the no less prepared effort of the other; and prayed only to be tried and acquitted, or condemned, according to the evidence contained in the depositions before the court, and not to be judged, by the tropes and figures of the counsel's heated imaginations. Mr. Maxwell he knew to be connected with the police, and with Josiah Hedden of the police. And he saw persons who from the gross expression of their features, he could perceive had been brought there to give circumstance to this malicious prosecution. He had not, he said, slept two hours during the last night, and he was not in a state to do justice either to himself or to those public men, who had signed that certificate upon which thank God, those gentlemen's names do not appear, nor did their character or standing entitle them to it. Not that man's, who libelled the greatest man we ever had in this nation, and who knew that the first and principal charge brought against him, was by a common felon. The heart he said must be base that knowing the merits of that accuser, could upon his faith, come here and utter such things as he knew must affect him and his family so sensibly. But if it was of no interest whatever to myself, I should stand up for that constitution for which my father fought: and I never will quit the subject while I have breath. For three hours I have had the knife of the assassin at my throat. Had this case been conducted with candor, it would neither have required the tongue of the interested traducer, nor rhodomontade, nor orotorical flourishes, nor reinforcements from Shakespear, nor the action of a Kean. I speak this of that counsel who libelled the best men in all this country, and though the honourable

Maxwell, and Martin S. Wilkins think me not fit to associate with them, I shall ask the aid of those who are as good or better; and who will not refuse to be associated with me. I shall show that it is not justice that is arrayed against me, but the coodies and intriguers of this city, who would trample me down. I am willing to resign my licence if it must be so; but I must insist upon the vindication of my reputation, and I will persevere in my efforts to defeat this malignant conspiracy to the end of my life.

The court, it being now six o'clock, adjourned over for an hour in order to give Mr. Niven time to collect himself, but did not think it proper to depart from the rule they had already made, that his three counsel should first be heard, and that he should be heard in reply. This arrangement had been made for his benefit, and proceeded upon accordingly.

The court having met pursuant to the above adjournment, Mr. Niven spoke at great length. He read the affidavits over, and commented paragraph by paragraph, his discourse occupied the court till midnight, when the court adjourned till 11 o'clock on the following morning, when he resumed and continued it till 20 minutes after 4 o'clock, P. M. having spoken nine hours, and 40 minutes and then presented the following written summary, which he begged to have placed on the files of the court.

To the Honourable, the Judges of the Court of Common Pleas.
GENTLEMEN,

With those proud sentiments that must ever govern the mind of an American, who esteems himself oppressed; and those virtuous feelings of indignation which prevail, when persecution is manifested, I present myself before you on this occasion I do so without fear, for my cause is an honest one. I do it without dread, for mine is emphatically the cause of the PEOPLE. I stand before *you* in the odious light of a peculator, summoned to the bar of justice; yet, to myself, I appear the defender of my country's honour, the protector of her laws; the suppressor of extortion, and the exposer of corruption. I stand before you a criminal, if honest integrity is a crime; and a peculator, if greedy and voracious extortion is a virtue. How I came to be here, is for others to infer; and what is to be the result, is for you to determine. If I prevail, virtue may claim a triumph; and if I fall, there is still virtue to subdue, and honesty to triumph over persecution.

It is now six months since proceedings were instituted to disgrace and destroy me, and though the result of malignity with some, and callous sensibility with others, it may not be amiss to give a history of their rise and progress. I saw the rights of citizens invaded; the constitution of my country assailed, and our laws made a pack-horse for private gain, at the expense of public oppression. I saw beneficent laws oppressively administered, and offices created for public good, perverted to an abundant source of individual speculation.

Perceiving this, and sensible of the results, I dared to express a decided censure where animadversion was due; and indignantly refused to tolerate, what, in my estimation, merited reproof. Fearlessly, therefore, my sentiments were conveyed, and I dared not only to utter, but to sustain them in a court of justice: thus I became an object of terror, and they sought to annihilate, in order to conquer, to recriminate, in order to destroy, and to intimidate, in order to avoid public censure, and public reproach. I have been represented by turns, as under the influence of partial derangement, or the dread of merited punishment; and my zeal has been ascribed to base and unworthy motives, instead of public good, and the preservation of judicial purity. I have been represented as the advocate of anarchy and the prostration of the law; the destruction of order and substitution of discord. All this availed but little, it was disregarded, for conscious rectitude controlled me in my actions, as well as professions, and my enemies were driven to procure by force, what could not be obtained by cunning. By one of those curious anomalies, of which my case presents a solitary precedent, I was presented by a grand jury; presented, for what, it is conceded, no man could be indicted, and for which, no man was ever before presented. My license as an attorney, detracts from my liberty as a citizen, and I am held to answer for *crimes* in the one character, which would be but immaginary in the other. It is sent from the Sessions to the Supreme Court, suspended over my head for nearly half a year, and then sent down for examination: Instead of "making my peace," as advised and succumbing to skulk from inquiry, I boldly invited a hearing; my conduct as a member of the bar had been impugned, and a sense of duty to the profession called upon me for a refutation, I met it promptly, and my defence was overwhelming.

Considering the presentment in the nature of an indictment, I was induced to believe that, having answered, I was entitled to a discharge, but in this I was disappointed; scarcely had my answers to the former depositions been read, before twelve more were ostentatiously spread before me; here let me beg permission to submit to the candid and unbiassed reflection of the court, the peculiar hardship of the case. I had been a practitioner at the bar, and for years engaged in a large and extensive business, in the discharge of my professional duties, I had, no doubt, incurred the envy of some, and the enmity of others; my occupation, from necessity, led me to a practice in the Sessions, and the defence of criminals; from this source, corrupt and depraved as it necessarily must be, from felons, and their participators, is a part of the evidence drawn, upon which I am seriously to be adjudged.

The constitution of the United States, guarantees, in all criminal prosecutions, the right of trial by jury, yet, in this, where the punishment to me is attended with consequence equally great, it is denied me. It stipulates, that the accused shall be confronted with the witnesses against him, yet, in this, to me important right,

I am disappointed. The affidavits against me have been secretly taken, they have received all the embellishments of language, and a miserable wretch, who it is proven is not to be credited under oath, a common vagrant, a pauper upon the community, and a vagabond, is made to pass as a merchant and a gentleman. It guarantees compulsory process for obtaining witnesses in his favour, and this too is denied me. I have placed upon the records of this court, an instrument covertly made use of to destroy me, a subpœna issued from the police office, by which an individual was made to testify, who otherwise would not have done so; a monstrous violation of what I conceive to be public duty. What! shall a man who holds a public station, exercise his office to legalise a proceeding as unlawful as it is vexatious? Shall he, by colour of his office, exercise the duties of inquisitor, be put into a situation from whence he may draw upon his own power, and through the influence and agency of retainers and agents, added to an assumption of authority, seek to destroy an individual whose hands are tied? It is not to be denied, that this prosecution was got up for the basest of all purposes; the satiating and indulgence of an implacable passion for revenge; I charge it so; it originated in the police office, and has required artifice and falsehood to sustain it; the justices of which, have become not only the preservers of morals, but have assumed the prerogative of protectors of the dignity of this court. I convicted one of them under the act to punish and prevent extortion, and if the channels of justice were of as easy access to me, as they have been to them, I should probably unfold a history that would make " even the angels weep."

Some of the affidavits relate to transactions that took place from four to five, and six years back; in the lapse of time, important documents have been lost or destroyed, material witnesses have died, and even with respect to proceedings of a more recent date, witnesses refuse to testify, though solicitously urged, suggesting that, as this is a police controversy, they don't like to interfere. Thus I have been deprived of important testimony which would corroborate, fortify, and render doubly sure, what must, notwithstanding, be considered as full and perfect refutation. Although, in this particular, I may consider myself unfortunate, yet I have every reason to rejoice, that by a kind of providential interference, documents have been preserved beyond what I had any reason to hope for or expect. This has been to me an important controversy, for as such I esteem it, not originating with this court, for I conceive them above participating in, or loaning the power of the bench to gratify the passions of resentment; but with the police, who have insidiously endeavoured to excite a prejudice both abroad and here, that would deprive me of a fair and impartial hearing. Josiah Hedden, whose finger has been unseen, has been felt, he has personally embarked in a contest, to recede from which he dare not, and to proceed he cannot, and which, in either alternative, will end in discomfiture and disgrace; he is governing, in conjunction with others, an effort to crush, which, in time, will re-act and overwhelm them, they will be viewed, by an abused and insulted public, with disgust and abhorrence. But truth, candour, integrity, and honour, must prevail, and honesty will ever triumph over chicane, intrigue, and deception; upon this principle I hope to attain an eminence among men, when such beings are crawling unseen, unnoticed and unknown.

To the members of the bar I cannot sufficiently express the sentiments of respect I personally owe them, for their liberality in proffering their support; in the midst of an unanswered and unexplained budget of matter, they volunteered an expression of fellowship and confidence. In the list of names which I presented to the court, will be found the weight of the profession; that document speaks volumes in my favour, and I appreciate the motive that excited, while I regret the necessity that urged such a document.

To our late sheriff, and those friends to whom I feel attached, for the decided, and unequivocal support I have received, I tender my grateful acknowledgments.

To the public I cannot do less than declare, that if I have errors, they are those of the head, and not of the heart, I sought to protect them, their laws, and the constitution of their country from being perverted to base and unwarrantable purposes; if I have not succeeded, it is because corruption has gained strength by combination, and a revolution is wanted in the system to come at the part diseased.

To the court within their personal observation, I may confidently say nothing has transpired to beget a want of confidence in either my ability or integrity, and as the evidence now stands, I am not only exonerated from the commission of any improper act, but I trust they will say suspicion itself is removed, by a complete, and fair, an honourable and overwhelming refutation.
George W. Niven.

The court adjourned till 2 o'clock on Saturday July 27, when the following Judges took their seats on the bench, in addition to the fiirst Judge. The Hon. Stephen Allen, Mayor, the Hon. Richard Riker, Recorder, and Henry Wyckoff, Elam Williams, James Hall, William Paulding jun. and Jacob B. Taylor, Esquires Aldermen. Alderman Fairlie sat on the first of June, but not after that day.

Opinion of the Court. George W. Niven, an attorney and a counsellor of this court, stands charged before us, with having received articles of household furniture and wearing apparel in pledge for his fees for professional services, proffered by him in cases where no professional aid could be afforded. Of having broken his trust in not applying the money of his client to the purpose for which he had received it, and of having decoyed off of the jail liberties a debtor who was imprisoned by virtue of a suit in which Mr. Niven was the attorney, with a view of affixing the surities of this debtor for the sum in which he was then held in execution.

It has been urged by the counsel for Mr. Niven, that admitting these charges to be true, they yet do not present a case which will justify this court in striking his name from its roll of attornies and counsellors. That he cannot in this manner be called to an account for the property or money he exacts or receives as a counsellor. That while the conduct of an attorney from his office being a place of trust, and from his frequently having the property of his client in his possession, may and ought to place him under the more immediate controul of the court, yet that the arts of a counsellor, who only proffers his talents as an advocate, and whose compensation is merely honorary, cannot be subjected to the same investigation and animadversion of the court.

An examination of the cases submitted to us, with others which have come under our own research, has satisfied us that all the officers appointed under the court, to and in the administration of justice are, when acting officially, subject to its authority.

Originally the parties to a suit attended court in person, and it was only by special statutes that they were allowed to prosecute and defend by attorney. By the statute of 3, Jac. 1. ch. 7, it was provided that those only should be admitted who "were well practiced in soliciting causes, and had been found by their dealings to be skilful and of honest dispositions." Various statutes have been passed in England since that period, as to the qualifications of attornies and solicitors, and regulating their examination, admission, and enrollment. The courts of that country have summarily punished gross misconduct, malpractice, deceit and misdemeanors committed by these officers, Cro. car. 74. 6 Mod, 187. 8 Mod 109. 2 Cowp. 829. 6 East. 140. Althouh the admission and regulation of barristers is not made in England the subject of statuary provision, yet it is laid down in Hawkins in his treatise of the pleas of the crown, that notwithstanding they are neither officers of any court, nor invested with any judicial office, but barely practice as counsellors, yet inasmuch as they have a special privilege to practice the law, and their misbehavior tends to bring a disgrace upon the law itself, they are punishable for any foul practice, as the ministers of justice are. Hawk. pl of the crown, 2 b 2. ch. 22. sec. 30.

In this state however, the legislature has not made any distinction between the different grades of the profession in regard to this admisssion. They are all examined, admitted, and enrolled. " If any counsellor, attorney, or solicitor is found notoriously in default of record or otherwise, guilty of any deceit, malpractices or misdemeanor, he may be suspended, or put out of the roll, at the discretion of the court." 1 Rev. Laws of N. Y. 416.

If guilty of deceit, or collusion, or consenting thereto, whereby to deceive the court or the party he shall be punished by fine and imprisonment, 1 Rev. Laws of N. Y. 417. And the same penalties are by a late act attached to his purchasing debts, and ch oses inaction for the mere purpose of litigation.

It therefore appears that there are abundant precedent and authority for this summary interference. Nor can we perceive any just reason, why a distinction should be made between the responsibility of an attorney, and a counsellor. They are both licenced by the court : nor can they engage in professional employment without its special permission. This permission can only be obtained by evidence of ability and integrity. Both are deemed requisite to a canditate for admission before he is considered worthy of being entrusted with the protection of the property, and the vindication of the rights of his fellow citizens, and it would seem to follow, that the same power which conferred ought to be authorized to withdraw this permission whenever those valuable purposes are abused.

If it is proper that our courts should enquire into the learning and moral character of applicants, for either of those grades, in order that a learned and upright bar may be entrusted with the interests of the community, is it not equally salutary that they should have the power to withdraw this sanction when it satisfactorily appears to them from the official misconduct of individuals in either grade, and their total want of integrity, that they are no longer worthy of public confidence. It would be strange indeed if this vigilance should be required only towards those who were passing the threshold of our courts, and that when once admitted, they should bid defiance to restraint, and with impunity be guilty of acts, which would have debarred their entrance. If the great purposes of justice, require this early caution and this careful examination, they still more imperiously demand the same watchfulness over those, who have been presented to the public, as deserving of their confidence and patronage. The power thus given to our courts is necessarily given. Its utility has been tested and sanctioned by experience. It should be discreetly but fearlessly exercised.

It has further been urged, that admitting the court to be possessed of this power, yet nothing has been established against Mr. Niven, which will require or justify its interference.

Mr. Niven, it appears was in the habit of proffering his services as counsel to those who were confined in the city prison, and from some of them who had not the ability to compensate him in money, he obtained articles of household furniture, and wearing apparel as a pledge for the fees required by him for these services.

From Frederick Stivers, who was committed on a charge of stealing, and after he had made a full confession of his guilt, Mr. Niven received a silver watch, a maple bedstead, and a mahogany table, to secure a fee of twenty-five dollars, for promised professional assistance. From William Charley, who was committed on a like charge, he in the same manner received a silver watch. From Alexander Kerland, who was committed on a charge of passing counterfeit money, he received his trunk of clothing in pledge. From Ellen Griffin a prostitute, confined in bridewell, and afterwards sent to the penitentiary, either as a vagrant or for disorderly conduct, he received her hat, veil, gowns and other garments in pledge.

Mr. Niven was also employed by Edward Couenhoven, to defend a suit which one Thomas Stevens had instituted against him in the Marine Court, of this city. At the time he was thus employed, he states that Couenhoven was indebted to him, in the sum of $21 and 24 cents, for services as an attorney in other suits which had been discontinued. Mr. Couenhoven was cast in the suit prosecuted by Stevens, Mr. Niven became his security to the court for the payment of this judgment, and received from him about forty dollars, for the purposes of satisfying it. Mr. Niven did not pay this money to the creditor, he retained it as he alledges to answer his own claims against Couenhoven. He was sued in the Common Pleas of this city, by Stevens on his engagement as surety He resisted and defeated this suit on technical grounds, and beside retaining the money he presented to Couenhoven a bill of costs for this last defence, amounting to $14 and 62 cents. Not having applied the money thus placed in his hands to the satisfaction of this judgment. Couenhoven was again called upon by Stevens for the amount, and had to pay it.

About two years since Mr. Niven had been professionally employed by a Mr. John Davenport, one of the butchers of this city, and at that time having a stand in the Washington Market. He recovered a judgment for Mr. Davenvort against one Bronson, the amount of which including Mr. Niven's costs, Davenport received. Mr. Davenport also had a demand against Mr. Niven, for meat sold to him, and there was a dispute between them as to the balance. Subsequently he was employed by a Mr. David Beadle, to collect from Davenport a debt. He commenced a suit against Davenport in Beadles behalf, prosecuted the same to judgment, and caused Davenports person to be charged in execution for this debt, Mr. Davenport gave security to the sheriff for the limits of the prison. While thus imprisoned, Davenport instituted a suit against Mr. Niven for the recovery of his demand, and which Mr. Niven resisted on the ground, that Davenport was indebted to him in at least an equal amount. While this suit was pending, Mr. Nivens brother arrived in this city. Mr. Niven having understood as he states, that Davenport sometimes went off the limits procured his brother to keep a watch upon Davenport's movements. Shortly thereafter, Mr. Niven, as he alledges leaving his brother in his office in Fulton Street, called upon Davenport at his stall, in the Washington Market, in relation to the differences between them. It had been agreed that these differences should be settled by the arbitrament of a counsellor of this court who kept his office at the foot of Dey-Street, and it was proposed that they should proceed to his office for that purpose. Davenport as he declares objected to going to Dey-Street, lest he should hazard the making his security for the limits liable. He alledges that Mr. Niven assured him, that while in his company as he was attorney for Beadle, the plaintiff, nothing was to be apprehended. Mr. Niven has not in his deposition expressly denied these assertions, but he declares that Davenport at first assented and agreed to go with him to Dey-Street. They however left the limits together, and while passing from Washington Market, through Greenwich-Street to Dey-Street, Mr. Nivens brother came from Mr N's office, down Fulton Street, to Greenwich-Street, saw Davenport off the limits, and immediately lodged process against the sheriff for an escape.

The differences between Mr. Niven and Mr. Davenport were not adjusted in Dey-Street, they returned towards the limits upon coming up Dey to Greenwich-Street, Mr. Davenport when about proceeding to Fulton-Street, the boundary of the limits, was induced by Mr. Niven to proceed up Dey-Street to Dawson's stables near Broadway, into which Mr. Niven went, and where they were for a short time delayed. They then proceeded through Broadway towards Fulton-Street, and before they reached the limits, were met by the brother of Mr. Niven, accompanied by a peace officer. The brother of Mr. Niven deposes, that his seeing Davenport off of the limits upon this occasion, was accidental, and not the result of previous arrangement. Samuel W. Jennings, however, deposes, that after this action for an escape had been prosecuted, Mr. Niven told him, that he had laid a plan to catch Davenport off of the limits, that he had succeeded, and that he gloried in it.

Such are the principal facts submitted to us in regard to the professional conduct of Mr. Niven. There are other matters which are also spread in the depositions procured against him, which we forbear to notice. We have only selected those which from all the depositions presented to us, both for and against Mr. Niven, are placed beyond dispute. They present, in our judgment, a course of professional conduct calling for the severe, and decided reprobation of this court.

We never can admit, that it is corrcet for counsel to receive from persons confined on criminal charges, their property in pledge for professional recompence. The abuses that may result from the toleration of such practices, are too manifest to require much animadversion. Independent of the frauds that may be committed upon those who appear from their situation friendless and forsaken, the practice in some cases may afford temptation to swerve from professional duty. If the pledge is great in value, and the fee to be secured by it bears no proportion to its value, and the accused is charged with a crime which may send him to the state prison for life, or expose him to a more awful punishment, his conviction, by depriving him personally of the power to demand or redeem his pledge, may secure to his advocate a greater reward than his acquittal. It is true, that after conviction, administration may be taken out against his estate, but the chances of such inquiries being set on foot for the property of a convicted felon, are too remote to be expected.

We consider, that in cases where individuals are confined, on criminal charges, destitute of money, and seeking professional aid, with a willingness to appropriate property to repay, or secure the services of counsel, the circumstances should be spread before the court, and their direction taken.

There never could be a hesitation by the court in adopting such measures for effecting this object, which humanity, and a regard to impartial justice, and the rights of the accused would require. A different course will lead to the most serious abuses, and the court may continually be called upon to settle the disputes between counsel and client, in respect to these pledges, their value, and their redemption.

These remarks we make in regard to the propriety of receiving any pledge of property in the cases we have mentioned. We shall not dwell, for we trust there can be no dispute on the impropriety of a counsellor of this court receiving the bedding, and the clothing of the imprisoned and the destitute, in pawn for his fees.

In regard to the case of Mr. Couhenhoven, we consider the appropriation by Mr. Niven of the money of his client, received by him for a special purpose, as a breach of his trust. This money was given to him to pay a judgment, and he had guaranteed its payment at the time limited by the court. Instead of delivering this money to the creditor who was entitled to receive it, he appropriated it to his own use. When sued, as security, he, by technical measures, defeated that suit, and then presented his client with a bill of costs incurred in a defence which he had not been employed to make, and in withholding moneys which had been expressly given to him for the purpose of payment.

In the case of Davenport, he admits, that his brother was employed to watch Davenport's footsteps. That Davenport left the limits in his, Niven's company. That advantage was taken by his brother of this temporary absence. That his brother opportunely came to the foot of Fulton-Street, immediately after he and Davenport had departed from the limits, and had but just time to go through the formalities of the law, in order to fix the sheriff with the escape, before the return of Davenport to the confines allowed him. Even were there no priority or arrangement between Mr. Niven and his brother, in regard to this transaction, it was glaringly improper for Mr. Niven, the attorney of Mr. Beadle, to pursue the bail of Davenport for an escape to which he had been manifestly an accessory.

The conduct of Mr. Niven, which we have detailed, and which is gathered from a careful review of all the depositions submitted to us, we consider as highly injurious to the character of Mr. Niven, and discreditable to the profession to which he belongs.

While correct conduct and fair dealing should distinguish every man in every department of life, we think it should be more especially required from those who, from their information and profession, are enabled often, with impunity, to take advantage of those whose interests are committed to their care. The counsellor, equally with the attorney, is entrusted with the protection of the rights and property of others. His power and opportunity, therefore, to do good or evil, is great. He may, by a course of correct conduct, become a highly useful member of the community. He may, by adopting a different course, perpetrate extensive mischief. The rich may be able to protect themselves, or pay for the aid of others against his breaches of trust, and his violations of confidence, but who is to protect the poor? who will stand up for those, the miserable remnant of whose property has been taken under the assurance of affording professional succor? It is cases of this kind which call more immediately for the interposition of the courts of justice. Apart from these considerations, the honour of a liberal profession is tarnished, when its members stoop to the shifts, and the expedients we have been considering, as the means of procuring a recompence for professional employment. However such practices may, by some, be considered as defensible on the ground of bargain and contract between man and man, we view them as disreputable, and as casting a stigma on a learned and liberal profession. It is the duty of our courts, as far as possible, to preserve integrity and fair dealing among those who are entrusted with the administration of justice. If purity should exist any where, it should exist in the seats of justice. If integrity should characterise any, it should characterise those who are engaged in its administration. The legal profession has a very considerable share of the public patronage. The various officers of trust, both in the state, and the general government, are frequently filled from its ranks. Its members form a large portion of the representation in our national and state legislatures; the best evidence of public confidence and regard. It behoves, therefore, our courts of justice, as far as practicable, to preserve this fair and honourable character. They owe it, not only to the community, to a conscientious discharge of public duty, but they owe it to the profession itself, to the learned, the liberal, and the honourable of the bar, whose character and usefulness are in some measure compromitted by permitting these disreputable practices.

After a patient hearing of every thing that has been urged by Mr. Niven or his counsel, after a careful examination of all the affidavits he has presented to us, in refutation of the charges preferred against him, we are constrained to say, that his conduct has been highly exceptionable, and though he has succeeded in exonerating himself from some of the accusations presented to us, yet sufficient remains to require from us, exemplary marks of our reprobation,

We shall direct certified copies of all the depositions and documents submitted to us, and of this opinion, to be forwarded to the Supreme Court, and our judgment is, that Mr Niven be suspended from practising as an attorney and counsellor of this court, until the further order of the Supreme Court.

Order of the Court, as entered on the minutes.

In the matter of George W. Niven, Esq., Gent. one of the attornies of this court, and a counsellor of the Supreme Court, on presentment from the grand jury.

A presentment of the grand jury, of the city and county of New York, accompanied with sundry depositions against the above named George W. Niven, as an attorney and counsellor at law, having been referred by the Supreme Court to this court for its consideration, and further depositions against the said George W. Niven, having been since submitted to this court, a day was given to the said George W. Niven to make answer in the premises. And the said George W. Niven having been fully heard in his defence, by counsel and in person, and this court having maturely considered all and singular the proofs and allegations as well for as against him, it is adjudged, by the court, that the said George W. Niven hath not truly and honestly demeaned himself as an attorney and counsellor at law, but on the contrary, hath in divers instances, imposed upon and decived clients, and other persons, whilst acting in his character as an attorney and counsellor at law. It is therefore ordered by the court, that the said George W. Niven be suspended from further practicing as an attorney or counsel of t is court, until the further order of the Supreme Court. And it is further ordered by this court, that certified copies of all the depositions and papers, which have been submitted to this court as well for as against the said George W. Niven, and also a certified copy of this rule together with the opinion of this court, be transmitted by the clerk of this court to the Chief Justice of the State, to the end that the same may be by him laid before the said Supreme Court.

Note Alderman Mead, met yesterdey and agreed with the above judgment. Alderman Depeyster dissented.

August 19, 1822.

This day an application was made to the court to make a final and positive decision by which Mr. Niven might be enabled to apply to the Supreme Court during the present term This was grounded upon an affidavit of Mr. Niven, stating, that immediately after the above order of suspension was made, the papers had been sent up to the Supreme Court at Albany, and a motion there made by Judge Van Ness as counsel for Mr. Niven, that the Supreme Court, all matters of form being waved, might consider the case as before them, and either make a final decision, or grant a mandamus to this court, upon the return to which the merits might be tried before them; but that the Supreme Court had refused to take cognizance of the case, saying they had nothing to do with it; that the court of Common Pleas must do as they saw fit, and that no mandamus could issue till that court had refused to do its duty, and letters from Judge Van Ness to Mr. Niven, were referred to as containing the information.

The First Judge. We understand that the Supreme Court have declined making any order till a positive and final decision of this court; but there are words in that affidavit which we do not think have proceeded either from the Supreme Court, or from Judge Van Ness, as containing an implication that this Court had not done its duty.

Some explanation took place, and the Recorder said, that if an affidavit was laid before them, that the Supreme Court had declined till this court had made a final decision, they should then have some basis to proceed upon; but if the Supreme Court had used any such expressions as implied that they had not done their duty, and they were conscious that they had, they must, then, of necessity, wait till they were coerced by authority. The Supreme Court would issue its mandamus, and they would make their return.

Mr. Niven then made affidavit to the effect, that he was informed, and believed, that the Supreme Court would take no cognizance of the cause till this court had made a final order.

The Recorder wished the counsel to write their motion down. The board of health were now in session below, and the majority of the judges might be assembled so as to pronounce an immediate decision, and give time for an application this term to the Supreme Court, there being yet a full week in term. A motion in writing was accordingly submitted by Mr. Niven, respectfully requesting a final decision, and in less than an hour, the first judge, mayor, recorder, and aldermen Wycoff, Williams, Hall, Taylor, Depeyster, and Mead, having taken their seats upon the bench, an order was made, grounded upon the above deposition and written motion, *that Mr. George W. Niven be suspended as attorney and counsellor of this court, for the space of one year from this date.*

Mr. Anthon then moved the court to make a voluntary return to an optional mandamus by consent of parties, to facilitate the application to the Supreme Court; otherwise, as this was the third week in which the term was prolonged for certain purposes by statute, it might not be possible to apply till the October term, where the court would sit in Utica; no return could be made till January, and perhaps no decision till May; so that the mere forms of proceeding might retard the final decision for a year. And Mr. Niven observed, that if the court had decided at first, he might have had a decision of the Supreme Court perhaps during this term, provided objections of form could have been got over, and he should not have been in his present predicament. The delay was that of this court, and the furthering of speedy justice would be rather complimentary than offensive to the Supreme Court. It would he said, have been better for him had he been at once struck off the roll; but if the court would consent to make this return now, he might get it before the Supreme Court on Wednesday, so that they might, perhaps, act upon it on Thursday. The present order, it was true, only deprived him of a branch of his profession; but this was an incongruity, for if he were really guilty he ought not to be allowed to practice at all in any court; and if he was still worthy to practice in the higher courts, he ought not to be prevented in the inferior ones. Nor could he well walk into the Supreme Court and try a cause as long as he was not thought fit or qualified to practice in a subordinate court.

The court said that they conceived the papers to have been sent back, because the time of the suspension had not been fixed; that is now done. How far it may affect or prejudice the party, or what course he may follow, as to practicing in the Supreme Court is not for us to say: but we know of no instance where the granting of a mandamus, by the Supreme Court has been anticipated.

Mr. Price, then moved that the first rule as entered upon the minutes be vacated.

The court considered that unnecessary, as it was superseded of course by the present order.

ERRATUM.

Page 32. last paragraph for my grandfather &c. read my father lived in this city, and descended with honour to his grave.

www.ingramcontent.com/pod-product-compliance
Lightning Source LLC
Chambersburg PA
CBHW032030230426
43671CB00005B/271